Yet Here I Am

Yet Here I Am

LESSONS FROM A BLACK MAN'S SEARCH FOR HOME

JONATHAN CAPEHART

GRAND CENTRAL

New York Boston

Grand Central Publishing
Hachette Book Group
1290 Avenue of the Americas, New York, NY 10104
grandcentralpublishing.com
@grandcentralpub

First Edition: May 2025

Grand Central Publishing is a division of Hachette Book Group, Inc.
The Grand Central Publishing name and logo is a registered
trademark of Hachette Book Group, Inc.

The publisher is not responsible for websites (or their content) that are
not owned by the publisher.

The Hachette Speakers Bureau provides a wide range of authors
for speaking events. To find out more, go to hachettespeakersbureau.com
or email HachetteSpeakers@hbgusa.com.

Grand Central Publishing books may be purchased in bulk for business,
educational, or promotional use. For information, please contact your local
bookseller or the Hachette Book Group Special Markets Department
at special.markets@hbgusa.com.

Print book interior design by Bart Dawson

Library of Congress Cataloging-in-Publication Data

Names: Capehart, Jonathan, author.
Title: Yet here i am : lessons from a Black man's search for home / by Jonathan
Capehart.
Description: First edition. | New York : GCP, 2025.
Identifiers: LCCN 2024057311 | ISBN 9781538767061 (hardcover) | ISBN
9781538767085 (ebook)
Subjects: LCSH: Capehart, Jonathan. | African American
journalists—Biography. | Gay journalists—United States—Biography. |
LCGFT: Autobiographies.
Classification: LCC PN4874.C246 A3 2025 | DDC 070.92 [B]—dc23/
eng/20250124
LC record available at https://lccn.loc.gov/2024057311

ISBNs: 978-1-5387-6706-1 (hardcover), 978-1-5387-6708-5 (ebook)

Printed in Canada

MRQ

Printing 1, 2025

For Mom

CONTENTS

Yet Here I Am

"I pretended to be somebody I wanted to be until finally I became that person. Or he became me."

—Cary Grant

CHAPTER 1

SONNY BOY'S BOY

My first vision of Willie Everett Capehart was a photo of him that sat atop the television console in the living room of my maternal grandparents, Joe Nathan and Isla Mae Kindred. He was in an open, flag-draped coffin. There was also a black-and-white picture simply dated 1967 tucked in a tattered photo album that shows my father sitting on a sectional in a white T-shirt, his left ankle resting on his right knee.

I always wanted to know more about him, the man who played a primary role in bringing me into the world, but whose contribution other than DNA remained a mystery. I was a middle-aged man when I learned my parents were introduced in Durham, North Carolina, in the mid-1960s. My father was a student at North Carolina College at Durham, Mom at Lincoln Hospital School of Nursing. They married two years before I was born and moved in with Capehart's mother in Brooklyn, where she settled after she left her husband and family Down South. "I was naive," a small-town girl who'd never really been anywhere, my mother told me.

Growing up, my mother made it clear that she didn't want to talk about him in general or about his death in particular. She was a master of conjuring silence. When I asked questions about my father, curt responses combined with an irritated and icy air would usher in silence as a third conversant. Stepping in like a burly bouncer to prevent the inevitable follow-up questions from entering the chat. The only definitive thing she told me was that my father died of what my young ears heard as "pulmonary embolous with infauction," but I'd later learn is pulmonary embolism with infarction. In plain English: Blood clots went from his legs to his lungs to his heart.

According to the obituary in a local paper, "He was employed as a sales representative for the American Oil Co. in Union [New Jersey], serving Essex and Union counties." The man called Sonny Boy by his family and Capehart by my mother and her family died at the age of twenty-six on Veterans Day 1967, four months after I was born.

What I did know about my father came from his father and younger brother, Granddaddy Willie and Uncle Johnnie. They made sure to remain a part of my life after Capehart died. A birthday card. A phone call. A Christmas gift. But the most enduring gift was our annual tour of Capehart relatives in rural North Carolina.

Pretty much every year until I was twelve years old, I spent summer vacation with my maternal grandparents in Severn, North Carolina. And each year, Granddaddy Willie or Uncle Johnnie would take me for a weekend of visiting the Capehart side of the family in and around Colerain, North Carolina, some thirty-nine miles south and east.

"This is Sonny Boy's boy," they would say, introducing me to relatives and my father's friends.

On sweltering front porches, inside fan-humming living rooms, and in the Gospel-rocking church where my father is buried, I was granted audiences with strangers who marveled at how much I'd grown, how much I looked like my father, how much I looked like my mother (if they'd met her), and how "book smart" I sounded as I answered their questions about school, life "Up North," and what I wanted to be when I grew up.

This was the 1970s, and Granddaddy Willie, who worked in the shipyards in Newport News, Virginia, and Uncle Johnnie, who was in law enforcement, were definitely men of that time, when gentlemen dressed up for such visits and topped off their suits with hats they removed before stepping onto a porch or entering a home. From them, I learned the theater of the social visit, the words employed upon arrival, and the language that signaled our farewell. They were handsome, charming, and their marital status notwithstanding, adept at courting female attention. It was not unusual to see either of them roll into the driveway in Severn for a quick visit accompanied by a beautiful woman who was usually questionably dressed for her country surroundings.

I was too young to ask thoughtful questions about my father or to remember many of the stories they told about him during those visits. Capehart remained a mystery. After I moved to

Washington in 2007, Uncle Johnnie sought to change that. By then, he was working at the Department of Agriculture and living in Maryland, and we would get together for dinner from time to time. One particular dinner stood out.

At Uncle Johnnie's Air National Guard retirement ceremony at Joint Base Andrews shortly after my arrival in Washington, my interest in my father was piqued. In his remarks, he took a rhetorical trip around the room to acknowledge the small group of attendees that included me and my mother, Margaret. When he got to me, his voice cracked, and his eyes welled up as he introduced me as his late older brother's son.

At one of our dinners, I asked about that moment. Why, forty years after my father's passing, were Uncle Johnnie's emotions so close to the surface?

He told me that my father was a man people talked to, sought advice from. He was always on the go, eager to discover the wider world he knew lay beyond the cotton fields of North Carolina. And it was my father who drove down from Brooklyn, where he was living with my mother, to pick Uncle Johnnie up at his college graduation to bring him back to the Big Apple. The way he reminisced, it was as if he were telling me what had happened just last weekend.

Uncle Johnnie loved my father when he was alive and especially after he was gone. He wanted me to know him, vowing to answer any question I had. His emphasis on "any" was akin to handing me a key to a vault filled with the answers to secrets. All I needed to do was use it, which I planned to do fully over future dinners.

Dropping me off at my apartment that night, Uncle Johnnie removed a brown paper-wrapped parcel from his trunk. He said he'd been carrying it for months so he wouldn't forget to give it to me. I waved goodbye, went upstairs, placed the package on the kitchen countertop, and went to bed. As I was racing around the next morning trying to leave for work, I realized I hadn't opened it.

Stripping away the paper, I took one look at the eyes peering back at me from the painting and exclaimed, "Who the hell is this?" It took a moment, but the answer was in those eyes. And as the realization swept over me, I whispered, "That's my father."

Recognition, but no connection. No childhood memories to tie me emotionally to him. No mementos of him that made him a daily presence in my life. No reminders that he had ever lived. Capehart's eyes peering back at me highlighted what I never had: a father.

My mother remarried when I was sixteen years old. When I first met the man, he was under our kitchen sink fixing a leak. I walked in to see him on his back, his legs moving as his hands fiddled with the pipe overhead. By then, Mom and I had our own language for talking about the man she thought worthy of me meeting. Awaiting a formal introduction, I must have said something to her that was characteristically smart-assed because she playfully smacked my shoulder. Looking at Mom in faux outrage, I asked, "Why'd you hit me?" But the response came from the giant under the sink. "It wasn't me!" His unforgettable defensiveness turned a playful mother-son moment into something more serious. A red flag I couldn't ignore. In private, I urged her not to marry him.

He was an arrogant man who had neither the looks nor the deep pockets that might possibly explain it. He had a capacity for meanness that saw him take every dime of my high school graduation money as payment for repairing a concrete wall that crumbled after I hit it with his pickup truck. Another time, in North Carolina, he took the $50 Granddaddy Willie had just given me for Christmas as part of the ruthless repayment plan.

Mom and I had repeatedly asked him to move two rifles he left propped up against the doorjamb leading to the basement. One night, I went to do my laundry. I couldn't see over the pile, so I felt my way around with my foot. My fumbling knocked one of the guns down, snapping it at the handle. He accused me of doing it on purpose. He said that the gun was given to him by his father and that it couldn't be replaced. But he worked out another plan that would kick in three months after my college gradua-tion. I would purchase a new gun that he wanted. It cost $348. I joked that he couldn't expect me to do that if I was working a minimum wage job. He thought I was serious and demanded the money right then and there. Tears silently rolled down my moth-er's face as she told me I had to pay him. It was the one time I saw my mother cry. All in a vain effort "to keep the peace."

My interactions with my former stepfather left me with the distinct impression that he thought very little of me. And with each interaction, I felt all of the self-confidence I'd had in abun-dance before moving into his house erode. During one pitched argument he told me that he hoped his young son, who didn't live with us, wouldn't turn out like me.

He thought my dreams of going into television news were just fantasies going nowhere. He had so little faith that he couldn't even pretend to see the investment I was making in my future when I accepted an unpaid internship at the *Today* show two summers in a row. He thought trooping to Midtown Man-hattan was a waste of time when I should be making money to help pay for college. As I left for the first day that second summer, he yelled from the second-floor bedroom to me on the sidewalk below, "No self-respecting college student would work for free for a second summer!"

From him, I learned how not to treat people. When something he did or said struck me as unkind or just plain wrong, I knew to do, say, or think the opposite. I've had plenty of father figures in my life. Uncle McKinley, Aunt Annie's husband, was the very definition of a good man. Like Uncle Johnnie, his love for his immediate and extended family, his love for me, was my beacon for how to be good. He was kind and paid attention to other people. I don't think it's a coincidence that most of the good men in my life are or have been married to very strong women. I pay as much attention to them as I do their husbands. They, too, are incredible role models of fortitude, confidence, and kindness. Their relationships showed me the importance of being your own person, of cheerleading your partner's accomplishments, and being supportive when things go sideways. Folks like Steve Lewis, the ninth president of Carleton College, my alma mater, and my first boss after graduation. And Tom Morgan, Carleton Class of 1949, who hired me as his assistant after he was appointed by Mayor Dinkins to run WNYC radio and television. Over the years, long after I no longer worked for them, both of these men and their respective wives, Judy and Hadassah, became surrogate parents. They stayed in touch, gave advice (solicited and otherwise), and let me know when they thought I was going astray.

And then there was Ed Gardner, a tall, elegant, old-school gentleman whose ties were fixed in place by a presidential tie clip given to him by President George H. W. Bush because of Ed's dedicated work as a trustee of the Points of Light Foundation. Ed taught me so much just by being himself, as did his wife, Arlyn. The glamorous couple loved to joke that they picked me up in an elevator. In reality, we were all leaving a mutual friend's holiday party on Manhattan's Upper East Side in 2001.

That short elevator ride led to a wonderful twenty-year friendship filled with monthly dinners, where Ed and Arlyn quizzed me on everything, from local and national politics to my personal and professional life. Over dinner in January 2007, we talked about the big trip I would be taking the next morning to Washington DC to meet with the *Washington Post* editorial board. Ed and Arlyn wanted to know everything. What was the job? How many people on the board? What would I be writing? Would I have to move to Washington?

Arlyn was certain the job was mine. There was no doubt in her mind. The same went for Ed. After hearing all my responses, he said something so moving that I was rendered speechless. "You're like my son so let me respond to you as a father." He then proceeded to tell me why I had to take the job if offered, how it was a stellar opportunity and that I shouldn't worry about leaving our beloved New York.

When I finally did speak, my voice quivered with emotion. It wasn't just what he said, it was how he said it. His words were weighted with love. They are a treasure, a prized possession that immediately settled in my heart. I've never forgotten them or how they made me feel. Ed was eighty-five years old when he passed away in 2020.

I am grateful to every father figure in my life, but I have always been aware that none of their love, care, and concern came with the parental responsibility of rescuing me if things got dicey. As a result, I often wonder what I've missed by not having a father and learning from him the lessons on how to navigate the world. To truly understand the expectations and advantages that come with being male, and the limitations and dangers that come with being a Black male. What did it mean that I grew up without having someone to call when things got dicey?

But I know, too, that Capehart would not have been the person to impart those lessons. He was in his twenties when he and my mother married. He didn't have the emotional maturity needed to raise a child, let alone hold a family together. A realization I was forced to confront after grief over Uncle Johnnie's death gave me the courage to shove aside the burly bouncer of Mom's silence to reveal a secret I never knew.

"Johnathan, pplease call the poolkice, something has happened to John."

Jeannie, a neighbor of my Uncle Johnnie in Prince George's County, Maryland, sent me that email on December 31, 2012, at 7:02 p.m.

At first, the misspellings and seeming incoherence of the message made me think it was spam. It wasn't until I received another email with her phone number that I understood it was real. When I got Jeannie on the phone minutes later, she was hysterical.

Uncle Johnnie had introduced me to Jeannie that summer. She was a neighbor and friend who wanted more, but their friendship seemed to bloom. Two weeks before Jeannie filled my ears with weeping, Uncle Johnnie took her to a White House holiday party. An invitation I was able to snag through my dear friend Jeremy Bernard, then the White House social secretary for President Barack Obama and First Lady Michelle Obama.

"Jeannie…got to shake the President's hand," Uncle Johnnie wrote in an email to me the day after the fete. "Of course she pushed people to get to him. The President [saw] her trying to get to him and he extended his hand to pull her through. She is so short, he probably thought she would get trampled."

"Jonathan & John, I did not push my way through to meet the President," Jeannie responded in her defense. "Yes, it was a great honor to shake (or should I say, to hold his hand) because it was a couple of squeezes (smile)."

The joy in that email was missing in the unexpected and painful phone conversation we had on New Year's Eve 2012.

Jeannie told me she called Uncle Johnnie to see if he wanted some sweet potatoes and the police answered the phone. She ran over to his house and saw him being loaded into an ambulance. The most vivid description she gave me of the scene she encountered was that "his arm was hanging off the side of the stretcher."

My call to Southern Maryland Hospital was grim. They only had his name. No other information. And as the next of kin on the phone with them, they asked for consent to give care. My repeated questions about what happened were rebuffed. The hospital official insisted that any questions would be answered in person. An impossible journey for me that evening. Just hours earlier, I was guest anchoring on MSNBC at the studios and was getting ready for another commitment in the city.

I was able to speak with Uncle Johnnie's ex-wife, who lived in Virginia. She told me that his pastor and brother were on their way to the hospital. Despite Jeannie's considerable fear and misgivings, I was able to convince her to go, as well. She and Johnnie went to the same church so she would know the pastor.

A little more than an hour after getting Jeannie's frantic email and call, the doctor called with the news I knew was coming. They tried everything, she said with the utmost care, "and we couldn't bring him back." The police had found him in his driveway unresponsive. EMS did CPR and other things after their arrival. I asked the doctor for the time of death: 7:25 p.m. He was basically gone when they found him.

Uncle Johnnie was the last link to Willie Everett, the father I never knew. The portrait of his brother that he gave me in the months before he died turned out to be a final gesture in what he had hoped would be among the many steps in turning a phantom into a father. My mother's reaction to seeing the painting was jarring.

I didn't see when she first saw it. I heard it. An unmistakable gasp. I turned in my chair at the dining table to see her stopped cold, staring at the painting with one hand over her mouth and the other in a loose pearl clutch. "I haven't seen Capehart in forty years," she mumbled.

The sadness I felt after Uncle Johnnie's funeral grew deeper over the next few days. I wasn't grieving properly. I was holding it all in. I felt gratitude for his love and care throughout his life. I felt guilty for not seeing him more often. The symptoms of the panic attack that had once taken me off an Acela train from Washington to New York in Wilmington, Delaware, nearly a year earlier returned to awaken me. It happened the night of Uncle Johnnie's funeral. It happened the night I learned the truth.

It was around 2:20 a.m. or so when I awoke and couldn't get back to sleep. My partner and future husband, Nick, tried to calm me down by holding me, telling me about the book he was reading. When the clock struck 4:35 a.m., I left Nick in bed for the living room sofa and called my mother. With tears streaking down my face and grief choking my speech, I poured out my sorrow. Then I asked her about the painting of my father.

"I wanted to rip it off the wall," she told me when I asked her what she thought when she first saw it. In my asking why, I was complaining that she never talked to me about him. About their marriage. About what happened. What she told me in those early morning hours was devastating.

Willie Everett Capehart abandoned his pregnant wife months before she gave birth in Newark, New Jersey. He took up with another woman in nearby Elizabeth, New Jersey. "I think your father came to visit a couple of days [after you were born]," my mother said. Those were the days when they kept mothers of newborns in the hospital seven days after childbirth. "He didn't stay long. I don't even think he held you."

Capehart passed away in a hospital in Union, New Jersey, which didn't inform my mother of his death until she called to check up on him later that day. No one called her. Not her mother-in-law. Not anyone in the entourage my mother complained he always traveled with. But one of his runnin' buddies, as Mom called them, would prove to be a guardian angel. My mother said a man came to the apartment in Newark and told her she needed to go to my father's apartment in Elizabeth and get all of his legal papers. Another guardian angel told her that she was entitled to Capehart's pension and survivor benefits for the spouses of veterans for the rest of her life. Thus, Capehart's desire to have his cake and eat it, too, to have a girlfriend without bothering to divorce his wife, turned out to be the saving grace of his callousness and changed the trajectory of our lives.

Recounting all this, Mom said everything she did "was for my baby." And she would repeat that phrase throughout our conversation, as if she were talking about a distant third person instead of the man that baby had become. I listened to her unspool the decades of hurt she had withheld from me. Now more than twice as old as my mother was when she trooped over to Capehart's apartment after he died, I began to understand why she never talked about my father. Why she flinched at the mention of him. Why she became a master of conjuring silence.

A few weeks later, my godfather, Joe Shambley, who was my father's best friend since childhood, answered an important question: Why did Capehart abandon us? Joe told me that my father loved to dance, and when the doctors told him that his blood clots required amputation of one of his legs, he said, "I was born with two legs and I'm going to die with two legs."

"He decided he was going to live a fast life until he died, and he did," Joe said. "He left Margaret before you were born."

CHAPTER 2

MY EDUCATION IN
JIM CROW

The weekend drive Down South from Newark always started early and was relatively fast. Mom would have us on the road before the spring sun cracked the horizon. "I'm only stopping for gas. So if you have to go to the bathroom, you better do it then," she would declare before every trip to my summer vacation with my grandparents in North Carolina. And she meant it. There was no shopping or supping at roadside diners like Aunt Annie and Uncle McKinley would do on their epic twelve-hour-plus drives from the Bronx. We would roll past the Severn City Limits sign five miles or so south of the lush green fields on the border with Virginia some eight hours later. Time was also of the essence since Mom had to get back to New Jersey for work on Monday.

My mom was born and raised in Severn, North Carolina, by Joe Nathan and Isla Mae. My grandparents and their seven children—five girls and two boys—lived in a simple, two-story four-bedroom house they bought for $3,000 from the local peanut company in September 1953 on an unnamed, unpaved street in the center of town. A town so small that you have to zoom all the way in on Google Maps just to make out the tiny layout of its streets. A town where Jim Crow was a prominent resident.

All around Severn are fields that burst in the summer heat with peanuts, tobacco, corn, and cotton. My mother and her siblings worked in the cotton fields when school was out, stuffing canvas bags with as much of the puffy fiber as would fit. On occasion, Aunt Elsie once reminisced that they would add water to their bags. More weight meant more money. Every cent helped.

Joe Nathan and Isla Mae married when he was twenty-three and she was sixteen. By then, Grandma had already had one child, my Aunt Lillian. A daughter Granddaddy raised as his own, who called him "Daddy" with such affection that it would be decades before I learned he was not her biological father. My grandparents' education stopped at grade school. They could both read and write and worked constantly. Joe Nathan hauled peanuts for the Severn Peanut Company, the major employer in town whose factory loomed like a corrugated metal Godzilla beyond his beloved pecan tree in the backyard. Granddaddy was a slim man of average height who always seemed to be clad in the blue uniform of the blue-collar worker, his dark chauffeur's cap snug about his full head of curly hair, until he entered the house or a store.

Granddaddy's voice was akin to a low growl, the kind I'd hear after the initial ignition of my Boxster decades later. Saying grace magnified its solemnity. One too many drinks increased his voice's volume and magnified its menace, as he alternated between rambling pronouncements and commands that we sit and listen. I always tried to slip from the kitchen, the preferred venue for his monologues, to the front porch, or any place out of his sight line. My little legs usually didn't move fast enough to be successful.

Grandma worked inside the peanut factory on the assembly line, plucking out the bad nuts from the good that came her way. When things slowed in the summer at the factory, Grandma would take the unpaved street from her house to the paved boulevard and sidewalks that led to the homes of white families that she'd clean. Homes that were visible through the morning mist from her backyard.

She was a zaftig woman with a proud bearing, a lazy right eye, an easy smile whose prominent feature was a big bottom lip that I inherited, and a love for Simplicity patterns. But Grandma always made the same thing: a sack dress that she slipped on with her arms raised in the air after her head went through the opening. The chrome kitchen table with its white enamel top and elaborate red pattern down the middle sometimes serving as a runway for my collection of toy airplanes or a track for my Matchbox cars was Grandma's sewing studio. Her metal scissors crunched on the tabletop as she cut her way across the tissue-papery pattern pinned to the fancy fabric. The Singer sewing machine hummed as she stitched the pieces together to reveal a creation she always thrilled over. She loved looking good, especially on Sunday, with her new dress, earrings, faux white pearl necklace, a little bit of makeup, and one of her wigs carefully transplanted from the Styrofoam head on her little bedroom dresser to her own.

Slowing down her convertible Mercedes 450SL to match the town speed limit on Route 35, my mother would take the first right. A perplexing habit to my young mind when the next right would take us right to her ancestral front door. Past Aunt Ercell's house, where daylight never penetrated its window shades. Past Aunt Essie Mae's with its screened-in front porch, where she would wave hello and call your name. Past the one-story, three-room shack where Aunt Annie was born. The growing family had moved there from their faded red shack behind the peanut factory they shared with Granddaddy's mother. Home now was the two-level, multiroom home closer to downtown, just on the other side of the freight train tracks where the post office, supermarket, and general store were. An old loading area near a commercial building became the end-of-the-day meeting spot for Granddaddy and his friends to talk, drink, and wait for me or my cousin Rita, my summer sibling, to come tell him dinner was ready.

But for my mother, that first right turn off Route 35 was defiance at 25 mph. Her slow roll down Main Street in her brown German ride with red interior was sending a message to the white citizens of Severn. The girl whose mother worked for them was home, now a woman with a Northern address and nursing degree. Once state-sanctioned discrimination was declared illegal, she was able to slip the educational and cultural limitations imposed by Jim Crow by earning a BA in special education from then-Kean College in New Jersey and a master's in audiology and communication from the same school in the years ahead.

My mother strongly believed that education was a prison key. If you grabbed on to learning, freedom and advancement were yours. Amassing as many academic credentials as possible, she believed, was vital for an African American to have a fighting chance of defying expectations and moving forward. But there was a catch. Because you're Black, you have to work twice as hard to prove you are just as smart as your white classmates. That meant sick days from school were rare for me, even when I had a cold. Not doing my homework was not an option. A's were expected. B's were tolerated. The rare C or lower was punished. No television, no friends until there was a turnaround on the next test or pop quiz. And there was no question that I was going to college. "If you're eighteen and not in college, you better have a job!" she would warn. "And if you don't have a job, you're not living here. I'm not taking care of a grown man."

Mom was tight with a dollar when it came to buying toys. But Washington, Lincoln, and Jackson always made an appearance at bookstores. Fairy tales, atlases, puzzle books, Agatha Christie novels, she indulged them all. I had two sets of encyclopedias. The colorful *Random House Encyclopedia* was a great addition in the late 1970s, although I did have to use it to prop up my mother's bed after some forbidden jumping broke off the left wheel from the box spring and mattress frame. She was none the wiser until she asked me a historical question neither of us could answer.

"Go get that *Random House* book," she said, sitting in bed with me at the foot. The dilemma was playing out in my head. She'd demand to know where it is if I said I didn't have it. She'd kill me if she knew her bed was broken. "Boy, go get that book," she said, half annoyed at my delay. So I bent down, lifted the blanket and top sheet with their nurse's corner still intact. The left front of the bed thudded to the floor as the encyclopedia appeared. We couldn't stop laughing. I, at having gotten away with it undetected for months. She, for not having noticed.

On the screened-in porch of my grandparents' house, where the sun rose at my back and set in a blaze of orange before my eyes, I would sit on one side of the green-painted wooden swing-for-two, my books on the other. I always brought books from home, and there were some at the house that I loved. The medical books with their plastic overlays showing the intricacies of the human body were fascinating. One summer, I found a history book on a small bookcase at the top of the sweltering stairs, so old that world history ended with the conclusion of World War I.

Rita was the pretty cousin who was Aunt Elsie's daughter but lived with Aunt Dorothy and Uncle Clark in Raleigh. Sitting on the swing where my books usually sat, she was like a daylily, the boys of Severn hummingbirds fluttering before her on the other side of the screened-in porch. They flirted. She giggled. I watched. The shirtless form of some of them stealing my attention. But they didn't seem to notice. To all of them I was "Mr. Peabody," the human version of the bookish cartoon dog that was popular on television in the 1960s and in reruns in the 1970s. And I was a little "funny." That was the gentler f-bomb used for someone believed to be gay back then. Although the time I emerged from the house decked out in one of Grandma's homemade dresses gave folks plenty of ammunition to believe perception was reality.

Summers in Severn were a glorious time, my country accent growing as thick as the grass we would run barefoot in. I used to take a broom to the dirt driveway to make an elaborate highway. Or it served as a runway. With my arms outstretched and the roar of the engines gurgling on the back of my tongue, a leap in the air was my takeoff and turbulence would shake my arms as I sailed higher.

Sometimes we would use our red wagon as a car, one of us pushing while the other used the handle as a steering wheel. Or one of us would sit in it and the other would pull, running as fast as we could, zigzagging along the way in the hopes of tipping the wagon over. One kid who was called Pumpkin—that's pronounced "pu'kin"—liked to come over and practice the moves from the latest Bruce Lee flick he watched on me. "Waaaaaaa! Ya!" He would scream, his flailing arms hitting my arms and chest, comically mimicking the sounds of the crashing blows from the movie, spit flying with every chop.

All of this was done under a blazing summer sun. Our skin, moistened by sweat and thick humidity, made for a slick landing pad for flies and mosquitoes that left itchy welts on our legs and arms. An especially juicy target was my head, denuded by a barber and his Number 1 clip. On really hot days, Granddaddy would attach the green hose to the spigot on the side of the house and then screw on the yellow multi-arm sprinkler. The cold water would whip out and up from the yellow arms, which whirled like the helicopter propeller blades. Dodging the dropped fruit of the pecan tree that loomed overhead, we would jump through the cool shower as we laughed, chased, and pushed each other around the yard.

Rita and I were not yet aware that we were enjoying our freedom as the first generation in our family to never have to pick cotton. Slaves bent their backs to pick it. Even after the Civil War that freed them, generations of their descendants—our parents, aunts, uncles, and distant cousins—continued their work for a pittance. Because of the Civil Rights Act of 1964, enacted exactly three years to the day before I was born, that duty stopped with Joe Nathan's and Isla Mae's grandchildren.

Jim Crow was legally dead. But its effects persisted. One summer, we arrived in Severn to discover the nameless dirt road that everyone called "Colored Street" had been paved. Not with the lush black asphalt that long made up the boulevard on Main Street, with its bold yellow double line. The newly paved and nameless road—it would be named South Street years later—was a blanket of small gray rocks mixed with tar that bubbled under the punishing summer sun.

For a town so geographically small, the psychological distance between the Black and white citizens of Severn was vast. From my grandparents' house to Main Street was a short walk. Shorter than walking from one end of Madison Square Garden to the other. But it was a world away. There was a wishing well on the "white side" of town. Really, it was water bubbling out of a spigot under a little gazebo that I'd slip over to visit. A sign promised that those who drank from it would return to Severn. The water tasted funny, a mix of rust and algae. No sign said I couldn't or shouldn't drink from the fountain. But town custom made my visit unusual, if not rare. Blacks drove on Main Street, but I never saw anyone Black walking on Main Street. Whites on South Street? Not that I ever saw.

It wasn't until I was older that I understood how important those summers in North Carolina were to developing who I am today. My views on race, my sense of place in the American story, took root there.

One of my favorite pictures is the one I took from that porch swing decades later. It must have been fall or winter because the lush green canopy of spring and summer is missing. You can clearly see in the distance the platform where Granddaddy and his friends sat before dinnertime, and the railroad tracks. In the foreground on the right is the side of the little warehouse where welding sparks could be seen shooting to the ground below. The entire scene is awash in morning sun. That was my view of the world, albeit with the summer sun in my face as it set behind the platform.

In my Hell's Kitchen studio apartment in the early 2000s, I mounted the framed photo on the wall opposite my bed. I wanted it to be the first thing I saw in the morning. A reminder of where I've come from. The humble origins of my family. The hard work of my grandparents. The de facto segregation the scene silently depicts. But the photo is also a symbol of possibility and progress. Sitting on the porch swing, I wondered what lay beyond the platform, the lives of the people in the places where the sun traveled after disappearing from view. The books at my side, the visits with the Capeharts, and my life up North gave me some insight. But as I looked at the photo from my little apartment high above Manhattan, it was not lost on me how far I'd come since those summer days. Living a life far different from the expectations of that small Jim Crow relic of a Southern town.

CHAPTER 3

JEHOVAH'S SUMMER INTERN

My real education in race came through religion. The dominant building in our view of the white side of Severn, North Carolina, was the brown brick, white spire, and stained glass Severn Baptist Church. Or "the white church," as it is known. On the other side of town, where Route 35 meets Water Street, is "the Black church," First Baptist Church of Severn. The Black church is perched on a hill that slopes up from the train tracks and was the church home of my mother's family in the early days. It is also the final resting place of Grandma and Granddaddy. But I would not set foot inside the place until my Aunt Dorothy's funeral decades later. Grandma converted to Jehovah's Witnesses sometime in the late 1960s or early 1970s.

On Sundays, we would make our way to the Kingdom Hall in Ahoskie, more than twenty miles away. Grandma was always at the wheel, unless Granddaddy decided he wanted to come. On the rare occasions that he did, the trip was much faster. What should have been a thirty-minute journey became an hour with Grandma, who drove under the speed limit and was afraid of tractor trailers, a terrible affliction in a region where they ruled the road. The sight of one coming toward her would have her slow down even more and hug the shoulder. One barreling up behind her would see her scoot off the road at the nearest turn or just stop as soon as she could, letting out her favorite exclamation, "Ah-WOO-whoooo," as it passed.

We were usually accompanied by Aunt Ercell, her sister who lived at the corner of Route 35 and South Street, the house perpetually shuttered from natural light. When Aunt Ercell would emerge from the side door, she always looked a bit disheveled, as if the sound of the car horn triggered a tornado inside her small home. She would then old-lady-waddle her way to the car and take her position on the bench front seat, her ample bottom hiking up to hit the headrest first so that she could slide into place. Just like Grandma. The view of Aunt Ercell from the back seat almost always featured a single gray-haired plat that stuck out from a wig she didn't quite cock properly into place. It always made me and Rita laugh.

Grandma's preferred route took her through Murfreesboro. From the back country road she traveled, she would make a left onto Murfreesboro's Main Street. The unemployment bureau, a sturdy, one-story brick building, was on the right. During the summer months, when Grandma was laid off from her peanut factory job until the fall, she would go to the cramped building's waiting area with me and Rita in tow to collect her check. After a left turn at the traffic light, Murfreesboro's main drag took us past the Belk's department store, the toy store, and other shops we would frequent. And then heading out of town was Hardee's, the charbroiled burger joint that introduced me to the tangy sweetness that comes with mixing ketchup and mustard. The vinegary aroma from Whitley's Barbecue on the outskirts of Murfreesboro would give way to the scent of pine trees wafting across Route 11, the two-lane highway that would bring us to Ahoskie's city limits.

At about ninety minutes, the Jehovah's Witnesses Sunday service was an efficient affair, the sermon a combination of reading the *Watchtower* and listening to Scripture being read by the minister. The night before Kingdom Hall, Grandma would have the *Watchtower* in hand, going through the lesson and hunting down the answers. It was like preparing for an open-book test where the minister could call on you for the answer. And there was singing. Just not the preacher-led, bring-the-house-down gospel singing of Southern Black churches. The devoted, like Grandma, were warblers: men, women, and children whose devotion to the mission of spreading the word of Jehovah outstripped their ability to carry a tune. I hummed when I wasn't using Grandma's pillowy upper arm as a resting place.

More importantly, there was witnessing, the act of knocking on a stranger's door and asking if they are interested in having eternal life.

Comedians get great laughs about this aspect of a Jehovah's Witness's life. But their jokes always had a city focus, folks ducking the Witnesses they didn't see coming up their sidewalk or in elevators. That's not how it was for country Witnesses like Grandma. Folks literally saw her coming as her car slowly made its way into their yard or up their long, dusty driveway.

Witnessing took Grandma all over the country roads between Severn and Ahoskie. She would even venture into Virginia sometimes. But no matter where she went, Grandma never made the mistake of rolling up to a white person's home to witness. The invisible walls that separated Black from white after slavery's end were hard to demolish in the minds of those Jim Crow left behind. You potentially put your safety at risk not knowing exactly where the barriers remained. After all, Grandma and Aunt Ercell witnessed near Nat Turner's backyard.

Southampton County, Virginia, where Turner was born a slave in 1800, borders Northampton County, North Carolina, where Severn is located. Turner's plan was to sack Jerusalem, the Southampton County seat, stock up on weapons and money, and abscond to the Great Dismal Swamp. Turner's rebellion started in the twilight of August 21, 1831, with the murder of the entire family that owned him. With the help initially of six other slaves and eventually joined by another fifty or sixty others, they slaughtered an estimated fifty-five people—white men, women, and children on eleven plantations—in a two-day blood-soaked rampage that unleashed fear across the South. But Turner and his fellow rebels never made it.

The Virginia governor sent troops and activated the militia to find them. Other whites got involved, too. By August 23, the bloodiest slave uprising in US history was squashed. Turner and the men who joined him scattered when the militia caught up to them at Belmont Plantation. Some were tried and sentenced to death. Others were immediately killed. Turner was the last to be found, two months later. He was tried, convicted, and hanged in Jerusalem, Virginia, on November 11.

Jerusalem had been renamed Courtland by the time Grandma and Granddaddy traveled there to get married four days before Christmas in 1940. They crossed the farmlands where Turner had unleashed so much fear and through the killing fields where Blacks were lynched and their severed heads hoisted on posts in retribution. Blackhead Signpost Road is six miles south of Courtland on Route 35. Another twenty-two miles south brings you to Severn. This is the terrain where Grandma sought converts to Jehovah.

Of all my experiences during those summers with my grandparents, going witnessing with my grandmother was the most indelible. Grandma Isla Mae only went to school until the fourth grade. That meant she could read, which was an obvious asset when witnessing to those who couldn't. The lessons I learned from her, though, weren't from any Scripture she read. They were by her example.

With her purse handle crooked in the bend of her arm, Grandma would climb the rickety steps of a weather-beaten home at the end of a dusty dirt road. We often found the folks who lived there sitting on the front porch, fanning away the heat or the flies and mosquitoes. Depending on the time of day, Grandma would say, "Mo'nin'," "Afternoon," or "Evenin'," followed by "How y'all doin' today?"

"All right," would come the slow-drawled response from the occupants, whose faces looked as old as their homes. Their eyes sometimes glowed yellow against their dark skin. The kind of yellow that comes from smoke, alcohol, and toil.

"My name is Sister Isla Mae. This is Sister Ercell, and this is my grandson Todd," she would continue, using my middle name that only my family uses. "And we're out spreading the word of Jehovah."

From there, Grandma would make her pitch. She would tell them how finding Him changed her life. How she looked forward to eternal life. Then she would ask, "Wouldn't you like eternal life without suffering in the Kingdom of Heaven?" Plenty of people told Grandma no, and she would take their rejection—they didn't believe in the teachings of Jehovah or they were fine with their Baptist upbringing—with equanimity. That doesn't mean she would give up. If one of the excuses was a lack of time, she would offer to come back to do Bible study with them another day more convenient for them. There was no waiting for those who said yes. Bible study started right there on the porch, or they invited us inside to escape the heat.

Grandma, Aunt Ercell, Rita, me. We all read Scripture and passages from the *Watchtower* and whatever book Grandma selected from the Brooklyn-based church. When she read, Grandma sounded like she was reading the lyrics of a song. Her voice reached for the right notes to match the majesty of the words or the lesson. Aunt Ercell was more of a staccato monotone, kind of like a disinterested flight attendant quickly narrating the safety instructions while her colleagues acted them out.

Shyness made me stumble over my words or read haltingly, something that occurs to this day. But I loved reading aloud. And in the process, I got to please Grandma by helping her in her mission. I could see how proud it made her. I also basked in the attention that being able to read gave me from those who couldn't. They told me how smart I was, guessing at what I would be when I grew up. Preacher. Doctor. Lawyer. While my family and strangers lauded my book sense, as I got older, some weren't afraid to decry what they said was my lack of common sense. Like being mindful that it was off-putting when I declined an offer of something to drink or shied away from anything dirty, especially when wearing anything other than my play clothes. Entering those homes during Bible study visits could be unnerving. Sitting on a dirty or dusty chair would occupy my every thought until we left. But those visits are burned into my memory for the living history they represented.

Inside, the houses shared common characteristics. They smelled old. The air hung thick with chewing tobacco and the exhaust of potbelly and wood-burning stoves. Their furnishings were minimal. They were free Blacks haunted by the remnants of slavery. The fields outside. The houses in which they lived. The deprivation that comes with being oppressed by laws and customs that denied their forebearers' freedom, made it illegal for them to read or write, and once freed, relegated them to second-class citizenship in the country they helped build.

But no matter how poor the homeowners were, whether their house was faded wood, standing tall next to trees that bore witness to history, or built from bricks, a sign of relative means, nestled underneath pine trees that laid a carpet of brown needles that crunched underfoot, their walls were universally adorned with an indelible pictorial trinity: President John F. Kennedy, Dr. Martin Luther King Jr., and Jesus Christ.

The presence of the Son of God was no surprise. He was our ancestors' North Star. After slavery, He remained their guide to salvation. I would learn over time who King and Kennedy were. How the former forced the nation to acknowledge that it had not lived up to the ideals laid out in the Constitution for African Americans. How the latter would send in federal troops to protect their civil rights at a time when the country was decidedly and violently against it. How his storied Camelot era was one of hope that a brighter day would come for them. It wouldn't be until I was an adult reading Taylor Branch's *Parting the Waters* that I learned why some of those homes also included a picture of Robert F. Kennedy. As attorney general, he was the one who pushed his brother, the president, to do right by Black folks striving to make this a more perfect union with every march, every Freedom Ride, every sit-in, every life given to that just cause.

Over the decades of remembrance, we have lost sight of who those Black folks who made history were. They were ordinary people who did extraordinary things. They had neither money nor fame. And they certainly didn't have any power. But they had the dream long before King articulated it. Their heroic efforts got this nation to live up to the stirring words in its founding documents. Ordinary people I read about in history classes and met decades later as part of my work. Ordinary people like the ones in whose homes I sat as Grandma tried to win them over to Jehovah.

These were salt-of-the-earth people who my grandmother taught me to treat with respect. They were "ma'am" or "sir." "Mister" or "miss." They were our kin, if not by blood, then by a tragic history that started centuries ago. Our appearance made it look like our circumstances were better than theirs. A socioeconomic sleight-of-hand aided by Grandma's perfectly placed wig and pearls and my crisp diction. But Grandma also knew very well that her circumstances were barely better than those to whom she was witnessing.

With each interaction with these elders, Grandma drilled into me a sense of humility. Not the kind where you downplay your skills or accomplishments, but the kind that guards against arrogance. I take nothing for granted, not the success I've achieved or the life it affords me, which serves me well in a world where the laws of gravity that many white people escape effortlessly apply doubly to Black folks. Good fortune can go south, and high public regard can plummet. Second chances aren't guaranteed. The benefit of the doubt is parsimoniously given, if ever.

Then, there is white envy of Black success. From an early age, I remember my mother and relatives saying some variation of, "They will only let a Black man rise so high or get away with so much or go so far." This belief was the foundation for every explanation of any scandal or hardship to befall anyone Black of prominence. Myriad examples of white envy of Black success abound in America. Wilmington, North Carolina, in 1898. Atlanta, Georgia, in 1906. The most famous manifestation of this is the destruction of Black Wall Street in the Greenwood district of Tulsa, Oklahoma, during a two-day white supremacist–led race riot in 1921. Protection of white womanhood in the face of false accusations of sexual harassment or violence was often the pretext for killing Blacks and pillaging their communities.

Over the ensuing generations, these experiences—and countless contemporary tragedies involving law enforcement and vigilantes—have made Black folks experts in white fear and insecurity. The fear of what white people are capable of lurks just below the surface of every Black person. No doubt some Black people will defiantly say, "I'm not afraid of white people." But nothing gets my racial spidey senses tingling more than a group of white men and/or white women out in public, especially if they are drunk. When their inhibitions are down, my flight instincts are on high alert. Despite brushes with raw racism, I didn't always think this way. For decades, I resisted viewing white people with suspicion like so many of my relatives and friends did. And it was all because of Miss Betsy.

———

Even after the demise of legal Jim Crow, Black and white neighbors came together in just two places in Severn: the Woodard's grocery store and the post office. Woodard's was the little grocery store just around the way from Granddaddy's platform, the place where I would buy cherry Blow Pops, sour apple gum balls, and big bottles of grape Nehi, as well as the Kool-Aid, Jiffy cornbread mix, flour, and other items Grandma would sometimes send me for that would find their way to the kitchen table.

The other place where de facto segregation took a holiday was the post office. Blacks and whites picked up their mail at the one-story brick structure where the American flag still flies high and proud. I loved turning the dial on the tiny bronze-colored box and pulling out the mail. Sometimes mixed in the bills and other notices for my grandparents would be a letter from my mother or a birthday card from another relative. Whatever interaction there might have been between Blacks and whites would have been respectful. That is, African Americans tried to display that they implicitly knew their place, and whites tried to ignore them unless absolutely necessary. But that was not my experience with Miss Betsy. She was a true Southern character, with a drawl like honey that spilled over even when she whispered on the phone.

Miss Betsy's husband was so filled with hatred for Blacks and Jehovah's Witnesses that she kept secret her change in religion and her friendship with my grandmother, who lived miles away. That was why we almost never went to Miss Betsy's home. That was why we knew who was on the other end of the phone when the caller responded to our hellos with just a whisper of where to pick her up. Her calls were always brief, like a spy reporting her location for extraction.

The rendezvous point was always in the dark middle of nowhere. A field on the other side of the road where a house sits next to a big tree at its bend. In a ditch near the railroad tracks somewhere. Depending on the location, Grandma would signal her arrival with a honk of the horn or a flash of her brights. And we'd wait. After a few anxious minutes, Miss Betsy would pop out from her hiding spot, walking briskly in the headlights toward the passenger door. We'd usher her in, making space on the floor of the back seat for her to hide if Aunt Ercell was in the front seat.

There was always a sense of menace as we made our way to a Bible study or the Kingdom Hall. As if Miss Betsy's husband would find his way behind our car and run us off the road or worse. Once we were a safe distance away and assured we weren't followed (which we never were), Miss Betsy would rise up to take up space on the back seat with me and Rita. She was always a mix of chatter and laughter and loved enveloping us in hugs. Her kisses to our cheeks were always wet from sweat and nighttime humidity.

Through her kindness and genuine love, Miss Betsy blunted whatever negative view of white people that could have taken root in my young mind during those summers in the de facto segregated South. She showed me that goodness in white people was possible. Life would show me that she was more exception than rule.

That's not to say that my childish eyes were blind to the ways of adult white people. Their undue suspicion, their dismissiveness, their soft bigotry of low expectations, if they had any at all. I saw it all. But I pushed back against it by viewing myself as equal, even if they didn't. After all, we were progressing beyond the bigotries of the past. I was born barely two years after democracy truly started to reign in America.

On Aug. 6, 1965, President Lyndon B. Johnson signed the Voting Rights Act into law. The Master of the Senate had Lone Star roots, giving him the gravitas to steamroll enough Southern Democrats for the votes required to make the laws on the books fully reflect the words and sentiments of our founding principles. The democracy that emerged made me part of the first generation of Black kids born into de jure freedom. And in the years that followed, from my childhood in predominantly white schools to my adulthood ensconced in predominantly white spaces, I viewed my role as an ambassador to the race. An interlocutor between Blacks and whites.

Through the relationships I built, I thought I was building a bridge of understanding. But matters of race are complicated. Some Black classmates and colleagues have called me a sellout, an Oreo, an Uncle Tom, a house nigger, perhaps even worse. Others don't view me as being "of the community" because I don't fit into their cramped hotbox of Blackness, a confining space whose boundaries expand and contract depending on whether you "belong." I have long called these gatekeepers the "Blacker than thou" crowd. Their sometimes-strident defense of Blackness in one case gives way to silence if the injured party is not "of the community." They can be doctrinaire in the demand for racial fealty by those outside their clique and maddeningly forgiving of blatant missteps if one of their own suffers the consequences of some transgression.

And yet way too late, I learned not every white person cared as much about my mission as I did. Way too late did I realize that Miss Betsy's transracial kindness might have only applied to me. Way too late, I realized not every white person is as comfortable with me as I am with them. Way too late, I understood that the more I defied the preconceived notions of what I was supposed to be, what I was supposed to accomplish in the eyes of many white people, the lonelier my world became. Suddenly, I was "intimidating." "Unapproachable."

Adding to that loneliness was learning out of necessity how to harden my heart to the pain from the microaggressions that pile up on any given day. The white women who have clutched their purses. The white men who have tapped their back pockets to see if their wallets are still there. The white colleagues who don't include me in the social life of the office. I have taken to loudly saying "Excuse me!" to white people walking on the wrong side of the sidewalk, but who invariably expect me to move out of their way. As an African American, I am acutely aware of the dark Jim Crow history of Black people being attacked or killed for not ceding the sidewalk to a white person. But I make sure my existence is acknowledged whether you want to see me or not.

The emotional toll of carrying this much racial baggage didn't hit me until the very end of a podcast interview with Robin DiAngelo. During the Trump years, I dove into trying to understand why white Americans were so susceptible to his racist ideas. I read three incredible books in near-rapid succession: DiAngelo's *White Fragility: Why It's So Hard for White People to Talk About Racism*, Carol Anderson's *White Rage: The Unspoken Truth of Our Racial Divide*, and Jonathan Metzl's *Dying of Whiteness: How the Politics of Racial Resentment Is Killing America's Heartland*.

Reading them in that order gave me a three-dimensional view of our rotted racial landscape. But what I love about DiAngelo's *White Fragility* is that she is a white woman writing unflinchingly to white people about race. She forces white people to get to know themselves, understand how white supremacy permeates their lives, and recognize how they perpetuate it. DiAngelo also dismantles the ready-made excuses and defenses white people use to absolve themselves of any responsibility when confronted with racism. She set the table for me to more fully understand the cyclical nature of "White Rage" outlined by Anderson and how that rage was manifesting itself in present-day America through policies that were leading people to choose their whiteness over policies that would help not only them, but also people of color as shown in Metzl's *Dying of Whiteness*.

Four days after the murder of George Floyd, DiAngelo and I had a frank conversation about racism and white supremacy and what white people can do to break its grip on our society. This is not passive work and shouldn't be left up to Black people to do it. I was wrapping up our interview when DiAngelo said something extraordinary.

"I'm going to look at you, Jonathan, in the eyes and say, on behalf of my people, I apologize," DiAngelo said. "I want you to know that as long as I'm alive, I will work to wake my people up, to continue my own process and to see that we can recover... And at least, when I am at the end of my life, I can say I did what I could." I cried. I had never met DiAngelo before and yet she intimately knew the pain that I carried. That she acknowledged it with utmost sincerity is what pushed me to tears. I was startled and moved and grateful, overcome with emotion because I was seen.

Being way too late in seeing the world as it is, being naive about what I thought was my unique role in changing it, is on me. Rather than waking up to the reality staring me in the face, I pushed ahead, thinking I could prevail over a system that had centuries of practice thwarting foolish souls like me. It was humbling and embarrassing to finally admit this to myself. And yet I have no regrets trying to live my values and live out my ideals. Ideals and values that Miss Betsy helped instill in me. My naivety gave me the blinders and boldness needed to plow obliviously through the bullshit to live the life I wanted to live.

CHAPTER 4

GROWING UP BRADY

The return of Mom's Mercedes marked the end of summer in Severn. By that late August date, I was ready to go home. Ready to leave the sweltering South. Ready to leave Bible study with Grandma. Ready to leave the tedium of picking butter beans or snapping the ends of string beans while *All My Chi'ren* and *Days of Our Lives* blared over the box fan moving hot air around the living room. I was ready to go back to having my own room in a high-rise in Newark.

Academy Spires, as they were called then, was home. Two 20-story brick behemoths that continue to sit off the southwestern edge of Newark's sprawling Branch Brook Park. A set of tracks where I used to place rocks and watch in amazement as the trolley crushed them separates the buildings from the park.

Interstate 280, the multilane escape route that allowed white flighters to bypass the troubles of Newark on their way to and from work downtown, underneath which a man sold the giant *Newark Star-Ledger* newspaper that Mom sent me to buy on Sundays when I was old enough, is a visual barrier between the Academy Spires and the rest of the city. A city rocked by riots sparked ten days after I was born.

Reverend Martin Luther King Jr. told Mike Wallace during an interview on *60 Minutes* in 1966, "A riot is the language of the unheard." And in Newark, one of the nation's first majority-Black cities, the white power structure that controlled government ignored the articulated concerns and needs of its Black citizens.

The bigotry, racism, and segregation that overtly ruled the South during Jim Crow manifested themselves in other ways in Newark. Substandard housing and education trapped Blacks in a multigenerational whirlpool of poverty. Blacks were not able to fully participate in the city's civic life. And police power was wielded as an instrument of white control in ways not unfamiliar to Blacks in the South. When I was born, Newark was gas-soaked kindling. A traffic stop in the evening of July 12 was the match that ignited it.

Cab driver John W. Smith was arrested by Newark police for a traffic violation and taken to the 4th precinct station house. The cops told the governor's select commission that Smith fought them in the back of the squad car and refused to walk when they got to the station house. They were forced to drag and then carry him inside. Smith told the commission that the police officers beat him in the back of the cruiser. The commission's 1968 report noted that Smith said he couldn't exit the car upon arrival at the police station and couldn't walk because of "a particularly painful blow in the groin."

For the Black people watching the scene unfold from their windows in the Hayes housing projects overlooking the police station, that was the last straw. Rumors of Smith's death at the hands of police drew angry crowds outside the station. It was a messy scene that descended into chaos after Smith was taken to the hospital. Molotov cocktails, rocks, and other projectiles were thrown at police. A truce negotiated between police and community leaders fell apart when police emerged from the station house sooner than the agreed-upon time.

For the next week, Newark's central ward was in rebellion. Fires and looting spread along Springfield Avenue and Clinton Avenue, South Orange Avenue and Bergen Street. The governor called in the state police. The National Guard was activated. A curfew was instituted. The riots—and the deaths and destruction that accompanied them—had a devastating impact on Newark. They were a punch that landed with such force that the city is still trying to fully climb to its feet a half century later.

That all happened after Mom brought me home to Apartment 20-I in Academy Spires. My mother and father had moved to the one-bedroom in 1966. The rough carpet was my earliest playground. I crawled on it. Mom played airplane with me on it, using her legs to hoist me in the air as I held onto her hands, giggling with outstretched arms. And I would prance across it from the kitchen to the bedroom on my tiptoes in the white-bottomed feet of my baby blue waffle-patterned pajama bottoms that were my imagined blue pantyhose.

Like my father, I didn't spend much time in 20-I. Most of the first four or five years of my life were spent in Upstate New York with my godparents, Callie and Joe Shambley. Before Callie and Joe moved with their daughter to a beautiful home with an apple orchard in Monticello, New York, they lived in Grahamsville, New York, in a trailer high on a hill among the many that rippled from Balsam Lake Mountain. Joe was a teacher at the local community college. Callie worked in an office. Together, Callie and Joe were strict and exacting, the embodiment of Black determination. They shared Mom's striving mindset. Doing your best was expected. No excuses were accepted for subpar performance in whatever you were doing, from yard work to homework. The former not being my favorite.

To get to their modest hillside home, you had to turn onto the steep road that led to it. Just hearing the opening notes of Chicago's "Does Anybody Really Know What Time It Is?" or the echoey serenity of Carly Simon's voice in "The Right Thing to Do" can transport me back to their black Volkswagen Beetle, where those songs played on the radio. The engine racing as it tilted its driver and passengers so far back, I felt like an astronaut rocketing to the moon on that lonely Upstate New York road.

One of their many visits to Newark to see Mom and me led to my going to live with them after my father died. "We were down to visit Margaret thinking we were going to see you," Joe told me in a long-ago phone call. "But you weren't there." He said Mom told them I was staying in Ossining, New York, with some folks related to my father. So they all jumped in the car to visit me. "When we got there, you were running around the front yard with nothing on but a diaper." They brought me back to Newark that day, and Callie and Joe gently asked Mom whether she wanted me to stay with her or would she allow me to visit with them for a while. Mom chose the latter. And there I would stay, learning the roads while standing in front of the Beetle passenger seat and gripping the handle on the glove compartment as the world unfolded in front of me. Learning the roads well enough to guide Mom from Newark to Callie and Joe's front door all by myself.

A little creek babbled under the tiny earthen bridge that allowed vehicles to cross from the road to the driveway. Their modest trailer sat in a clearing that was bathed in sunlight on cloudless days. To think of the place now is to smell the woods after a good rain. That rich, humid smell of green and dirt. The yard sloped down to a thicket of trees in the distance where friendly white neighbors lived on the other side. A yard where, on more than one occasion, I was instructed, "Go get a switch!" And then watched, frightened, as the leaves on the wisp of a branch were shucked off. The power of something so slight to inflict such pain became clear as the whistle of its approach was drowned out by the repeated screams of "I'm sorry!" as it whipped the skin on my legs, butt, and thighs. The number of welts on my arms depended on how vigorously I fought to grab nature's lash to lessen the impact of the coming blows. But Joe was not parsimonious with praise, and Callie was not stingy with enveloping hugs.

When I returned to Academy Spires to live with Mom, she had traded our one-bedroom apartment for a corner two-bedroom one floor down. From my own bedroom in Apartment 19-J, the night lights of Newark, alternating between brown and orange, pale green and white, glittered in the distance, depending on where you looked. Cars streaked across 280, and planes flew to and from Newark International Airport.

After a summer of wearing shorts and living the life of a Jehovah's Witness, I returned to a life of school uniforms and

Catholic instruction. St. Rose of Lima was my elementary school, a ten-minute walk from home and an even shorter distance from United Hospitals, where Mom worked as a nurse in the pediatric ICU.

Kids would play on the closed-off street at St. Rose until we were called to assemble and then give over our day to the stern nuns waiting inside. What they lacked in warmth they more than made up for in the private education they gave us. Our parents were paying for us to learn what was not being taught adequately or well in Newark's public schools. But as I went from one grade to the next, my mother's anxiousness grew.

By my tenth birthday, we had left Newark. Conditions at Academy Spires had deteriorated. The neighborhood wasn't the safest, and temptations for the young son of a widow were all around. Private school tuition climbed with each grade. With high school approaching, the bill promised to be prohibitive, assuming your application passed muster and you were granted admission. If not, you were at the mercy of Newark's public schools. To that, my mom essentially said, "Nope!"

North Plainfield, New Jersey, was a startling two-year pit stop. We went from a predominantly Black city to a predominantly white town. From an apartment building to a development of split-level apartments, the kind where each building unit had two apartments stacked on top of the other. Once through our front door, we climbed stairs to get to our two-bedroom home that had a sizable balcony made unappealing by chipping paint that crunched underfoot.

As a child of the Jim Crow South, my mom was always on guard and tried to prepare me for what could happen now that we were living in a town where we were sure to be one of the only

Black families around. The racism experienced could be casual. Like the girl in the downstairs unit who dubbed the rhythm and blues coming from our radio in the morning "jungle music." And the racism could be overt. The walk from West End Elementary was less than a mile and featured a pedestrian bridge over an always-bustling Route 22. One afternoon, as I walked along West End Avenue toward home, I looked down a street where I saw a car of what looked like teenage boys in the distance. One saw me and yelled, "Let's get him!" I ran, fast, my overstuffed book bag slapping my back with each frantic step, pushing me toward and over that pedestrian bridge. And out of danger.

North Plainfield is also the place where the gayness I tried so hard to hide made a very public debut. I begged my mother to come get me from a YMCA New Year's Eve sleepover because the sight of the hairy bush and lengthy penis of an older boy stopped me in my tracks. My trance was broken only by the laughter when a boy said, "He looks like he wants to suck it."

Mom and I did not like North Plainfield much. Years later, she would tell me, "It was like going from a Black ghetto to a white ghetto." So I was thrilled when we moved to a new residential development in Hazlet, New Jersey, called Village Green, just off Exit 117 on the Garden State Parkway. This was 1979, way back when what is now a massive Home Depot parking lot was a working farm whose owners would sell their produce from a nearby roadside stand.

My most cherished childhood memories originate from this suburb twenty-four miles south of North Plainfield and light-years away from Academy Spires in Newark. There was nothing special or remarkable about our townhome. There was a powder room on the ground floor, where we also had enough space downstairs to create a den area, which was needed because Mom was from the generation where the living room was populated with furniture that neither I nor my friends were allowed to sit in. That space was meant for company.

Upstairs were our bedrooms. Mine faced the front, where tenants parked their cars. That's how I learned to distinguish between the hum of our fuel-efficient Honda Civic and the low growl of mom's Porsche 944. Hearing the latter signaled Mom's return home. Sometimes it would send me scrambling to stop doing something that would prove blindingly embarrassing if caught. Other times, it would induce waves of relief. She was safely home. Aware that I was the only child of a widow, I lived in constant fear that I was one accident away from being an orphan.

Mine was a childhood filled with more television viewing than was recommended. I consumed countless hours of local news, national news, and those one-minute network news breaks that hit just before the top of the hour. The locations of stories taking place all over the world would send my eyes to the maps that covered my walls. They ranged from *National Geographic* glossy to the simple paper design sent by foreign embassies upon my request, first for a book report and then to feed my newfound obsession with geography. I wanted to see where the action was happening.

When I wasn't watching the news, I was glued to *The Electric Company* and *The Mickey Mouse Club*, *Speed Racer* and *Battle of the Planets*, *Bugs Bunny* and *Scooby-Doo*. *The Six Million Dollar Man* and *The Bionic Woman*. I loved them all. But none more so than *The Brady Bunch*. I had seen every episode so many times, I could name the forthcoming storyline within the first few notes of the music that played after the theme song.

One episode in particular made a lasting impression, the one where Marsha and Greg run against each other for student council president. And then the opportunity presented itself at Beers Street Elementary School. I was the new kid and the only Black kid in my seventh-grade class (if not the entire school) when the teacher asked, "Is anyone interested in running for vice president of the student council?" The student body president was always an eighth grader.

How I wanted to raise my hand, to be like Greg and Marsha. But I was too afraid. Whatever inner turmoil that beset me then gave way to joy as I turned to see the white kids behind me pointing in my direction. Maybe they thought putting the new Black kid up for election was the ultimate prank. Maybe I was setting myself up for failure by agreeing to run. Who knows? Who cares? I won.

Hazlet was where I played tennis on the courts at Village Green. A hobby I picked up during Mom's tennis phase, when the older African Americans told me I looked like a young Arthur Ashe. Where I did gymnastics in Alison Fiala's backyard. She was Mary Lou Retton and Nadia Comăneci to my Kurt Thomas and Ron Galimore. We loved gymnastics so much that we performed at the school talent show. Clad in white tank tops, blue polyester shorts with triple white piping on the sides, and rainbow-striped *Mork and Mindy* suspenders, we tumbled and flipped across the tiny stage to *Hooked on Classics*. We ended by jumping into splits. I jumped so high and landed with such a thud on the stage that I'll never forget seeing every boy in the audience grab his groin as a collective howl of "OWWW!" rumbled from the contorted faces of their hunched-over bodies. Such acrobatics earned me the nickname "Iron Balls."

Hazlet was also where I began to learn how to be Black in white spaces. Blackness is always at the mercy of someone else's judgment. You can be too Black, not Black enough, or not Black at all, and I have run the range my entire life. Some Black people are eager to take away my Black card. Some white people would rather I not mention my race at all.

I was playing with my friends near the tennis courts at the other end of the apartment complex. I don't remember what we were talking about exactly, but we were laughing, telling little jokes. What I do remember is my contribution to the levity. "Well, I'm going to carry my Black ass down there," I said, employing a bit of phrasing common in Black households and utterly unfamiliar to my white friends. "What does race have to do with this?" one friend snapped. Nothing, specifically. And everything, culturally.

They had no idea what "Black" meant in that sense. To them, I was invoking race where it didn't belong. To me, I was treating friends like family. In our families, "Black" is used for comedic effect or to put an exclamation mark on a warning. Mom, like all Black parents and relatives, was adept at the latter. "Don't you EVER, as long as you're BLACK..." was a favored preface for one of Mom's admonitions against doing any number of offenses. "Black ass" is used in multiple ways, especially to grab one's attention. One of Mom's favorites was "You better bring your Black ass here right now!" or "Your Black ass is gonna get left if you don't hurry up!"

My use of "Black ass" was clearly comedic. But in feeling comfortable with my white friends, I violated an unspoken agreement with an unspoken expectation: I was not Black at all. The burden was mine to glide effortlessly between my Black home and family to the whiter world. To switch from down-home vernacular to precise language devoid of anything ethnic. The tacit agreement required that I live on their terms. Back then, before the introduction of the Walkman and long before the MP3 revolution, there was no way to bring the R & B of WBLS that was the soundtrack of my home life on the bus ride to Raritan High. The speakers of our glossy yellow chariot blared the rock music of WPLJ.

The rules of the unspoken agreement are designed for maximum white comfort with Black presence, which means we must constantly prove to white people, especially those who don't know us, that we are following their rules. Hence, my mother's mantra that is the mantra in every African American household: You have to work twice as hard to be considered just as good and just as qualified as "them." If you are ever considered such, know that it comes grudgingly. And even then, the whiter world will remind you of where it believes your place to be.

Before my first day at Beers Street Elementary School and at Raritan High School, my mom sternly told me not to let "them" put me in vocational education classes, that "they" liked to push Black kids into trade schools instead of college. If anyone tried to deter me from college prep classes, I was to tell her immediately. Given my grades, I was decidedly on the college prep track. But on the first day of classes at Raritan, I discovered my homeroom was in the shop, known as the place where burnouts, troublemakers, and non-college-track kids were sent. My desk was a big table around which sat several students. The stool I sat on was right next to the table-mounted metal vise. At the sound of the first-period bell, I raced away from the smell of freshly sawed wood and metal to join my fellow nerds.

Another reminder came my sophomore year, during a meeting with the high school guidance counselor. For weeks, our regular instruction had been interrupted by those tests that required sharpened Ticonderogas to fill in those maddeningly narrow ovals and teachers to yell "pencils down!" when time was up. Those were IQ tests, the counselor told me. "You see this number," he said, pointing to a number I no longer remember. "That's your IQ." He told me that the low number suggested I would not get into college. But he said he was baffled because my coursework and grades suggested otherwise. From then on, assessment tests filled me with dread.

A lot of what I did in upholding my end of the unspoken agreement was about the perennial adolescent need to fit in. About being an only child who was the new kid in a new school—and a Black kid in a white school, at that. When you are that kid, you become adept at navigating the unspoken agreement. I got really good at it and started believing I was special. A notion my mother sought to dispel when I was about thirteen.

My next-door neighbor and best friend was Skip, a cute sandy-haired boy of divorced parents who skied the Matterhorn every Christmas with his TWA pilot father. Together, we led a merry band of mostly white hide-and-go-seek/Risk/tennis-playing nerds. Mom had long warned me that if I were called "nigger" at school or at play to tell her immediately. She was not going to put up with that kind of Southern hospitality anywhere near her or her child. So when someone dropped the N-bomb as we played outside the apartment, I raced inside to alert her. After she dispersed my little friends from our back door, she came inside, sat me on the sofa in the den, and delivered the inevitable reality check.

"Right now, you and Skip are here," she said, holding her hands in front of my face at the same level. "But as you get older, you won't be equal." Her hands now visually separated, she continued, "He'll have advantages that you won't because he's white." Her words landed with the force of punches from Muhammad Ali. I thought my mother was being cruel, a prisoner of the past. Her Jim Crow upbringing did not jibe with my multiracial post–Civil Rights present.

With tears streaming down my face, my voice grew hoarse as I loudly and repeatedly screamed, "No! That's not true!" And I demanded, "How can you say that?" Mom tried to calm me down while assuring me that I would one day see the truth in her words.

The simple racial hierarchy revealed by my mother failed to mention the gradations of recognition and respect applied by whites to Blacks. Some were worthier than others, as I learned sometime later from a classmate who thought she was paying me the ultimate compliment. "There are Black people and there are niggers," she said. "You're a Black person."

When you are trying to fit in, any positive nod to your existence is joyfully received. But her declaration recognized my individual humanity, while it denigrated the rest of my race. She set me apart partially because I worked twice as hard to be seen as just as good. But she also set me apart because I clearly had mastered the other unspoken rules of the unspoken agreement. Perfection—from grammar and diction to grades and grooming—was what society required of me, not just what my mother demanded of me.

Defying the stereotypes seen nightly on television is every Black kid's burden in that world. So in word, speech, and dress, my childhood in the 1980s was one big "I'm not like that" act of separation. I played tennis and did gymnastics for fun. I played the flute at Beers Street and the oboe at Raritan. I ran for student government and won. I got along with everyone. I loved my classes and my teachers. Life was great.

Then we moved back to Newark.

CHAPTER 5

FRESH PRINCE
IN REVERSE

In Hazlet, I had a great group of friends that traveled in a pack. We played tag and tennis, rode bikes, and roller-skated. We went to each other's homes. I knew their parents and they knew my mom. My student council electoral success and the popularity that I enjoyed in elementary school repeated itself in high school.

Despite the low IQ I supposedly possessed, my science teacher took me and a bunch of other overachievers who were not in her AP biology class under her wing. After school, she taught us what she was teaching the brainiacs in that class, the highlight being the exciting and gruesome task of dissecting a fetal pig. The smell alone disabused me of any desire to go any further after finding the pre-piglet's liver. Because the teacher was so kind, it was only natural that I turned to her to discuss a personal emergency. My mom was getting remarried.

The announcement took place in the den. I found my mother and Mr. "It wasn't me" seated on the sofa after my mother called for me to come downstairs. As I stood before them, they told me their news. Not only would they marry, but Mom and I would be moving back to Newark to live in his house. I can only imagine how the shock rippled across my face as I looked at the man who would soon become my stepfather.

Mom had dated other men. Men to whom I gave nicknames. My favorite was dubbed "Kermit," after the lead in *The Muppet Show*, that Mom and I never missed. He was a handsome, smart, kind, and quiet man. When their relationship ended, Mom and I were both bummed. Into the void came the oddly defensive and arrogant man, whose nickname I no longer remember.

Through gritted teeth, I said, "Congratulations," and left the room devastated. I would be leaving a town I considered home and the friends who helped to make it so. But a terrifying thought sent me racing back to the newly betrothed with an urgent appeal delivered as a demand.

"You're going to have to find a private school for me to go to," I said with a dash of defiance. "I am not going to public school in Newark. I'll get beat up." And with all the Dominique Deveraux drama I could muster, I departed—again.

The prospect of going to public school in Newark felt like an existential threat. First to my education. After all, my mother had moved us out of Newark six years earlier mostly because of that city's deteriorating public schools. But also, a move back felt like a threat to my safety. I was Steve Urkel long before the Black nerd with the big glasses, high voice, and high-water pants showed up on American television in 1989. It did not help that I did gymnastics or played the flute. I feared that the snickering

I sometimes endured in predominantly white schools could give way to more physical efforts to challenge my "nonconformity" at a predominantly Black and brown high school. No, I needed to go to a private school. My physical and educational well-being would be protected there. This was the internal teen turmoil that tumbled out to my science teacher. Her response came in the form of a question.

"Have you heard of St. Benedict's Preparatory School for Boys?" she asked. "It's a wonderful school." She told me that her husband used to be a monk and taught there and that she could help me get an interview. Next thing I know, my mother and I are waiting on the wooden pew-like bench in the quiet vestibule of St. Benedict's. The unhurried monk in full Benedictine habit with a rope belt who made his way past us did not break the silence. If anything, it added to my terror. This interview had to go well. I had to get into St. Benedict's. The tuition was not so onerous as to make the school out of reach. Its eleven-month school year spoke to a rigor that would be missing from Newark public schools. When I was accepted, it was a relief. But it did not solve all of my problems.

My mother and I moved from our suburban two-bedroom town house condo to my stepfather's foursquare house in the Weequahic section of Newark—about a mile from where the literary great Philip Roth grew up. The once-middle-class Jewish neighborhood had become majority Black since the riots and the white flight of the 1960s. The house sat near the top of Meeker Avenue, a wide sycamore-tree-lined street that sloped downhill to Elizabeth Avenue. The thoroughfare had seen better days, but its longtime middle-class Black residents, including my stepfather, took pride in their homes. The little patches of grass in the front were routinely mowed. In the spring and summer, I sprayed down the sidewalk and front steps. In the winter, I shoveled both and the driveway before getting ready for school.

I will say this much—the house inspired care and devotion. Coming from our little place in Hazlet, the 1925 house felt grand. Except for the kitchen, the entire first and second floors were covered in wall-to-wall emerald green carpeting. Set against crisp white walls, the lush flooring made the house's high ceilings soar. The large living room had a working fireplace with high-back chairs on either side. Chairs that were moved for the wedding ceremony in December 1983, but were back in place that time Carl and Betty came over to help broker a peace between Mom and my stepfather.

The sunroom was my favorite. Three of the four walls in this jewel box were windows where sunlight would sometimes trickle through the curtains. I camped out there during their courtship, and after we officially moved in, I could be found there, pretending to lead a life infinitely more glamorous and serene than my reality. On the second floor were the master bedroom, where Mom and my stepfather slept, and two guest rooms, which never actually hosted guests. There was also the main bathroom, the place I hated cleaning the most.

The heart of the house was the kitchen and its table, the place where my stepfather held forth amid the organized chaos of the place with the television on, the phone nearby, and mail all around. The place where I made the mistake of leaving my diary, which he read and questioned me about, saying he would keep it for future reference. He gave it back a week later. At that table, I ate fast. The faster I ate, the faster I could get away. The negative implication of this survival tactic was brought home to me during a dinner in a hotel ballroom while attending a Youth in Government conference. I looked up from my finished-in-no-time-flat plate to see a young girl seated at our table looking at me with wide eyes. With great sincerity, she asked, "Would you like mine?" Mortified and in no need of her charity, I declined. The faster I ate, the sooner I could start doing the dishes. A forty-five-minute nightly chore that went by quickly because my mind drifted elsewhere. Once finished, I would escape to my room on the top floor, up the stairs where my stepfather had thrown dishes I'd once neglected to put away. Among the dishes was a butcher knife pointing straight out over the stairs.

When Mom and I moved in, not long after I finished my sophomore year of high school, my uniform was basically tennis whites with the collar popped. This was the 1980s, after all. But my stepfather warned me that I would stick out like a sore thumb in my new urban environment. He advised me not to leave the house dressed like that. We were barely there a week when his warning proved correct.

I wanted a snack, but there was nothing snack-worthy in the house. So I decided to head out, stepping into my new neighborhood for the first time dressed like I was heading to Wimbledon instead of to the corner store at the bottom of the hill. Sure, I felt self-conscious, but I was the only person on the street at that late-morning hour and made it to my destination unbothered. With my soda and snack in hand, I started making my way back up the hill. And then things took a turn. Suddenly, there was an arm around my neck. An insistent voice from another direction demanded, "Drop the bag! Drop the bag!" All the while, I was being shaken to and fro. I didn't want to lose my snacks. And I most definitely didn't want to lose the change from the $20 bill that lay at the bottom of the bag. But I gave the thieves what they wanted. Whatever was left of my sense of security was decimated when I saw my assailants running away. Three Black kids a little younger than me.

My return to Newark went about as well as could be expected. I was a Fresh Prince of Bel-Air in reverse. A suburban middle-class Black kid who grew up playing with white kids now back in a majority Black city with no clue about how to relate or fit in. More accurately, it was as if the Fresh Prince's preppy nerdy cousin Carlton Banks had moved to the neighborhood. The only difference between Carlton and me was that he was fictionally clueless. I was the one who was clueless enough in real life to get mugged in broad daylight.

When I recounted the events to my mom and stepfather, they reacted with concern and were glad that I was not harmed. Still, neither could suppress their "that's what you get" smirk. But what happened that morning terrified me. So much so, that I did not leave the house again without one or both of them with me for months. That meant on the first day of school and every morning for a few months after that, I was driven to school, usually by my mother.

My notions of prep schools were nurtured by *The Official Preppy Handbook*. They were wealthy white institutions where the boys dressed well and played lacrosse or tennis on their manicured campuses. While that might have been the reality at Andover or Lawrenceville, that was not my reality in the middle of Newark.

St. Benedict's Preparatory School is a Hope-sized diamond in Newark's battered crown. Founded in 1868, the private Catholic school that educated boys from the seventh grade through high school was an academic force in New Jersey's largest city, producing business and civic leaders. At first, the school on High Street (changed to Dr. Martin Luther King Jr. Boulevard in 1983) was the domain of German immigrants, then Irish, then Italian. In the 1970s, St. Benedict's made a concerted effort to admit Black students from the Black neighborhoods around it. But the 1967 riots that raged right outside its doors hastened a decline in white enrollment that forced the revered school to close its doors at the end of the school year in June 1972. Almost immediately, the Benedictine monks set about devising a plan to reopen the school. Part of their commitment had to do with a fealty to the community around the school. But I do not discount the impact of the experiences some of the monks had while studying at St. Bernard Abbey and College in Alabama in 1963 and 1964. There, they saw the depravations, desperation, and separation that ruled countless Black lives in the segregated South.

St. Benedict's reopened on July 2, 1973, under the brash leadership of Fr. Edwin Leahy, a twenty-six-year-old graduate of the institution who by his own admission "had no training...and absolutely had no plan." By the time I arrived ten years later, he and the monks had devised a 7–12 school with the intense academic rigor of its storied antecedent. I was the nerd who loved school and homework back in Hazlet, but even I was knocked back by the deluge of homework during the eleven-month academic year. The standards maintained by the monks and the lay staff were high. Excellence was expected. Anything less than that demanded an explanation and an acknowledgment of the expectation of improvement. What was *not* tolerated was giving up. "Benedict's hates a quitter" is a school motto.

The monks and Fr. Ed, affectionately called "Fred" by some students, also created a school that was very much part of the African American community around it. For many of the boys admitted, St. Benedict's was an educational and societal refuge from the tough homes and neighborhoods they lived in. Neighborhoods that still bore the scars of the riots that tore Newark apart. Sure, some of my fellow Gray Bees came to school weighed down by more than the books in their backpacks. That's why another school motto is so powerful: "Whatever hurts my brother hurts me." Combined with "Benedict's hates a quitter," the two mantras form the foundation of a strong cohesive community of empathy, humility, and mutual respect.

Easy for me to see that now. It didn't feel that way for much of my time there. I was a new kid in my junior year in a school where most of the boys had known each other since the seventh grade. Students are divided into groups of boys from all grades that stay together the entirety of their time at Benedict's. They were a family. I gained a gaggle of stepbrothers who didn't know what to make of me.

Each morning, I popped out of a Porsche with my tennis racket nestled in its Gucci cover as I leaned hard into the preppy part of my prep school appearance. Inside Benedict's, I was an oddball. Not that I was the only one. One student named Brett looked, sounded, and dressed like Michael Jackson, right down to the red leather *Thriller* jacket and the single glove. He became one of my closest friends. Our affinity was also based on what we recognized in each other, not that we tried to hide it or could if we wanted to. Perhaps we talked about our attraction to men.

I do not recall. But if we had, I know I extolled the virtues of Tom Selleck's hairy chest, Rob Lowe's beautiful blue eyes, Shaun Cassidy's feathered hair, the sexiness of Erik Estrada and Larry Wilcox in their *CHiPs* uniforms, the sleek physique of Lorenzo Lamas in *Falcon Crest*. The list was endless. There were snickers about our friendship, but that did not make me shrink from him. I stand by my friends.

Another close friend was Charles "Chuckie" Whigham III. Maybe we became friends because we both were junior-year newbies in a school filled with boys who grew up together. But I wanted to be his friend because he was what I aspired to be: handsome and rich. Chuckie lived with his grandparents above their funeral home just blocks from school. The Whigham Funeral Home is a Newark institution that handled the funeral services of Whitney Houston after the megastar Newark native died in 2012. The same institution that handled my father's funeral decades earlier.

The beauty of St. Benedict's was the absence of the "wanna-be white" stigma that envelopes Black boys and girls in public schools who excel or want to excel. As if academic excellence and whiteness were the same or inextricably linked. In those High Street halls, excellence was all around, and it was predominantly Black. Brett, Chuckie, and our classmates were there to learn and to meet expectations set by the monks and our families. I was always confident and comfortable in the classroom. But not in the halls.

Fr. Ed didn't help matters. As Thomas Allan McCabe noted in his history of St. Benedict's Prep, some students had "a love-hate relationship with him." I, too, had a love-hate relationship with him. There was a spring trip planned for a small group to a convent in Cuernavaca, Mexico, that was billed as a two-week excursion into poverty so extreme that we could be staying in mud huts. Spots were limited so you had to apply to go. Figuring it would be a trip of "Fred" favorites, I never thought I would be selected. But at the meeting for the chosen few, Fr. Ed went around the table telling each boy why he would be going. When he got to me, he said, "I chose you because I want to see you up to your neck in mud."

Another reason for my discomfort outside the classroom was of my own making.

Chuckie and I both had experience navigating predominantly white spaces. But he came from a prominent and wealthy Black family. This brought him racial and socioeconomic street cred that put him on a whole different plane. I was a pretender. With every drop-off at school, I projected an elevated socioeconomic standing that did not exist. We were not poor, but we were not rich or socially connected to the Black elite, either. Mom was not a member of The Links. My stepfather was not a member of The Boulé. I was not part of Jack and Jill. We were a middle-class family that engaged in aspirational pursuits. Mom had a tennis phase and a short-lived golf phase. She took me to the ballet, the symphony, and to hear the great Leontyne Price perform at Carnegie Hall. When Mom remarried, my stepfather's outdoorsy pursuits took over. There were the rides on his Harley-Davidson, fishing trips in his bass boat, and camping trips. I only went on one. So ill equipped was I for the entire experience that I packed actual suitcases. And if surviving the first night's rain and high winds was not enough, the communal bathrooms swore me off the activity for life.

We didn't join the cavalcade of middle- and upper-middle-class Blacks to Sag Harbor on Long Island or Martha's Vineyard, that gem of an island floating off the coast of Massachusetts during the summer. We headed to my stepfather's mother's house in Wildwood, a beach community near the southern tip of New Jersey. He drove a tow truck for the local Sunoco gas station once his teaching duties were over. With a modest number of properties, he and his family acted like they were the Helmsleys or the Trumps. Above-it-all and better than everyone else. My step-grandmother was as grand as she was mean. A retired schoolteacher, she spoke with perfect diction and precise language, especially when cutting you or someone else down to size. Her home was tasteful and meticulously maintained. Her bedroom was arranged in such a way that from her bed she could see into just about every room on the first floor through an intricate layout of mirrors that started in her master suite.

My junior and senior high school summers were spent on the second floor of that house. A small room across the way from Mary, a lovely and perpetually wary-looking woman who was not related to my stepfather or anyone in their family. She kept to herself and had the cautious mien of a houseguest striving never to impose herself on her hosts, even though that house had been her home for years by the time I took up my Sunoco summer residency. And it was while staying in that house that I came face-to-face with racism in two incidents that left an indelible impression.

The Sunoco was perfectly situated to watch the weekenders flow into town from Philadelphia, surrounding Jersey communities, and Quebec, Canada, interestingly enough, and to take care of their cars on their way out of town. In New Jersey, you cannot pump your own gas. That was the job of the gas station attendant. My job. At first, I hated it. Really hated it. The dirt, the grime, the gas tanks of cars that sometimes belched the fuel all over me like milk from an overfed baby. It took me a while to learn, but when it got busy, I could fill up a tank in one car, wash the windshield of another, and still have time to check the tire pressure of a third.

It could be grueling and dispiriting work, given the way people treat those they are paying for service. But I loved the feeling of accomplishment that came when the shift ended. It also didn't hurt that I made a lot of money in tips for cleaning windshields. One guy gave me a dollar tip because, he said, "I've never seen anyone take such care in cleaning a windshield." You are damned right I took such care. There was no way someone as fastidious as me was going to clean a windshield and leave water streaks anywhere on the glass.

Between the tips and my meager minimum wage paycheck, I was able to open an account at a local bank, where I made a point of asking for the same bank teller. She was pretty and kind to me, so nice during each visit. Over time, our friendly chatter increased. And then I asked her out.

Joan Rivers was one of my favorite comedians. She always cracked me up when she filled in for Johnny Carson. So I jumped at the chance to see her live in Atlantic City, especially since the show was on my eighteenth birthday. I just did not want to go alone. The only friend I had in Wildwood was that bank teller, so I nervously waited in line to ask her to go with me. Much to my surprise, she said yes. After all, I was a Black teenager and she was a young white woman probably in her twenties. But the announcement of my plan was met with a ferocious response from my stepfather (and his mother) and led to a pitched yelling and screaming match between me and him.

He wanted to know why I was taking "that white woman." He said she would spend all my money while keeping hers. He wondered aloud about the prospects of being run off the road by some rednecks. In a fit of narcissism, he complained that he would have to deal with the senility of my mother if something were to happen to me. For good measure, he said that he hoped his biological son never turned out like me. He repeatedly demanded that I not take the young woman. And each time I refused—until he threatened to get her fired.

He did not know her or anything that mattered about her. He did not know how her kindness made this shy, awkward kid smile. He was denying me a friendship because of her race. There were lots of assumptions of what would or could happen if I took her to the show in Atlantic City. It was like the Skip conversation Mom had had with me years earlier. The one where she calmly explained the racial facts of life to me and I howled in disbelief. I was still the naive child, but this time the emotional reactions were being directed at me. It was like I went from being not Black enough in Newark to being Mandingo in Wildwood. Centuries of ancestral experience enveloped their raw reactions. I know and understand that now. Although at the time, I felt like I was talking to people trapped in a painful past. But the past is not the past for people with lived experiences who fear present-day consequences. The unrelenting pressure to change my mind succeeded. I disinvited the bank teller and took my Aunt Elsie instead. In some ways it was the perfect outcome.

Elsie is my mother's younger sister, the third-born of her six siblings. She settled in Atlantic City in 1962 after graduating high school, and when the casinos arrived, she went to work at Caesars Boardwalk Regency. She was a waitress at the Hyakumi Japanese

Steakhouse and loved every minute of it. She loved the work and her colleagues. And she loved her customers. She remembered them and their quirky preferences and they loved her back. And how could they not? Her joy for life was so over-the-top that when I first saw the movie *Auntie Mame* starring Rosalind Russell in the title role, I instantly thought of Aunt Elsie. Mame's message to Agnes Gooch was Elsie's mantra to me: "Yes! Life is a banquet and most poor suckers are starving to death!" She grabbed life by the horns and wrested whatever happiness she could from it. And she wanted to make sure I did the same.

Spending my days off from the gas station with her was my light at the end of the tunnel of that summer job. The hour-long bus trip filled me with as much joy on the ride up as it did with dread on the return. The Sunoco job had its charms, like the little bench in front of the shop window, where I sat waiting for customers. In the morning, I plopped down a pile of newspapers on my left. In the evening, a coworker usually plopped down on my right. I nicknamed him Popeye because, clad in his blue mechanic's uniform with the sleeves rolled up, the squat, older white man who had the build of someone who was quite buff when he was younger, looked just like him. He cursed up a storm. He was gruff. He was wonderful to me. Never more so than when I came under attack.

From that little bench, we were taunted by the golden arches of the McDonald's across the busy roadway. The hungrier I got, the more abusive the ocular relationship became. One night, the lull in business made it possible for me to dash through the stopped inbound weekend traffic into McDonald's. Food in hand, I attempted to go back the way I came. A pickup truck of young white men had other plans. They were not content to just yell racist epithets at me. They sped onto the gas station's lot, chasing me into the shop. As Popeye hurled verbal brickbats, my stepfather waved them off with an actual bat.

I was nothing to the thugs who set upon me simply for being Black. They did not know about my good grades, my killer two-handed backhand, or the stack of newspapers that demonstrated my intelligence and curiosity. They could not see me because I didn't exist to them. I was nothing more than a punching bag, an inanimate object on which they could unleash their frustrations and insecurities without fear of consequences. We called the police. Nothing came of it.

That experience was the first of many that would later prove to me that my mother was right. Education and money offer no real protection from racism. Both give you the illusion of control. A nicer job. A nicer home in a nicer neighborhood. A group of similarly situated friends and family (blood and chosen) who know the tightrope you are walking because they are walking it, too. And they are there when that illusion of control is breached. It always is. Racism is a monster that neither drowns in your deep pockets nor asphyxiates in the rarified air of your soaring career. The monster never dies. You learn how to survive despite its pernicious presence in your life.

For two summers, I sat on that gas station bench watching the world go by as I dreamed of a life that would allow me to do the same. A dream that started to become a reality my freshman college summer.

CHAPTER 6

A DESTINATION WITH NO ROAD MAP

There was a name for kids like me. The kids who couldn't stop talking and loved telling other people's business. We were called tattletales. My big mouth got me in big trouble during one of those North Carolina summers and led to an ongoing, nearly fifty-year silence between me and the aunt to whom I mailed a letter informing her of her husband's infidelity. The consequences of that juvenile revenge ended my career as the family blabbermouth, but it kind of explains my love of news. An obsession that started when I was about ten years old.

I must have been out of school because I was staying at my Aunt Annie's and Uncle McKinley's apartment in the Bronx. I recall McKinley telling us to turn on Channel 4, the NBC station in New York, to watch the *Today* show because they were broadcasting from the plaza and he would try to get in camera range to wave. Instead of looking for him, I became fascinated by the countless correspondents who told other people's business on television from all over the world.

My love of geography grew out of this. I would consult the dozens of maps that blanketed my walls to see where the action and the correspondents were. The world became more fascinating as I married the stories with their locations, the unfolding current events with their underlying histories. The more I learned about the world, the more I wanted to be a part of telling its myriad stories. I told anyone who would listen that I wanted to be a "news commentator."

Tom Brokaw and Jane Pauley were the *Today* show anchors when I started watching, but it wasn't until Bryant Gumbel, the Black NBC Sports anchor, succeeded Brokaw in 1982 that I saw someone who looked like me doing the job. I never doubted I could do the job or would be given the opportunity to do so. Explicitly and implicitly, my mother never put limits on my ability to achieve anything. Sure, she warned me about the obstacles I would face, but the word "can't" never followed "you." Still, the obstacles were many. Chief among them was not having anyone in television news or journalism or a writer of any kind in the family. I had a destination, but no road map to get there.

The closest I came was my Uncle McKinley, an electrician at NBC's 30 Rockefeller Plaza headquarters for forty-one years. He was the guy you called for everything, from a short in a socket to replacing a light bulb. That put him in all parts of the art deco masterpiece in Midtown Manhattan. One morning in late 1984 or early 1985, after my Carleton College interview at the New York Hilton a few blocks away, I asked if I could drop by

30 Rock, the nickname for his workplace long before the hilarious Tina Fey–Alec Baldwin comedy made it common knowledge. McKinley never said no to a visit. He had gotten used to me swinging by to roam the floors, hoping to catch glimpses of news sets and the anchors I watched on television. I loved slinking around the sixth floor, where *The David Letterman Show* and WNBC's *Live at Five* studios were. The halls crawled with staffers and stars, generating an internal excitement that was rocket fuel for my desire to be in the mix when I grew up.

McKinley was leaving the workspace where he and his colleagues gathered when I arrived. Something needed to be done in one of the *Nightly News* offices, and he asked if I wanted to come along. A rhetorical question since he knew the answer. And as we made our way to the suite of offices on the third floor, my mind raced with the possibilities. I thought for sure that I would be walking into an area buzzing with broadcast news giants like Brokaw or John Chancellor. Instead, the office was virtually empty, except for a lone woman sitting at her desk. Her paper coffee cup was the classic blue-and-white Greek diner kind, and her bagel sat atop the brown paper bag it came in. And spread before her was one of the New York tabloids. From the sofa where McKinley told me to sit and wait, I stared, working up the courage to talk to her.

"Excuse me," I asked finally, "do you work here?" She did, indeed. Her name was Ann Skakel Terrien. Then, she asked the question all adults ask kids: "What do you want to be when you grow up?" With this question, I learned what would become a life-long lesson. When someone asks you what you want, tell them. And I told Ms. Terrien everything. How I wanted to be an NBC News correspondent in Moscow. How I was trying to decide if the next move should be to the London bureau for more international experience or to the White House to cover the president. How I loved the *Today* show. How my ultimate goal was to be the next Bryant Gumbel.

My torrent of oversharing was interrupted by McKinley's announcement that it was time to go. I thanked Ms. Terrien for talking with me, and as I started to walk away, she said, "Wait a minute!" Reaching into her desk, she pulled out a notepad with the NBC logo at the top and wrote down a name, Kay Bradley, and her phone number. With a flourish of her hand, Ms. Terrien handed me the note and said, "Here! Get yourself an internship on the *Today* show!" I did as I was told. I contacted Kay Bradley, the show's no-nonsense program coordinator who had a hand in picking the summer interns. And I was picked.

For two summers, I made my way from Newark to 30 Rock. I could get from Newark Penn Station to New York Penn Station easily. My New Jersey Transit train ride was usually spent standing by the door so I could quickly get off the train once it rumbled its way underneath Madison Square Garden. I had been on the New York City subway many times. Always with Aunt Annie and Uncle McKinley riding to stops in Harlem and the Bronx. But I didn't really know how the subways worked in Midtown Manhattan. So I walked.

Emerging from the warrens I had once traversed as a kid with my mom to and from Knicks games, I walked as fast as I could over to Sixth Avenue and up to the studio. The goal was to be standing in Studio 3B in time for the 7:30 a.m. open of the *Today* show. I wanted to know what happened behind the scenes. As Bryant Gumbel and Jane Pauley opened the show, I watched John Palmer settle into his place at the news desk on the other side of the studio. Once Bryant and Jane threw to him, I watched them move to the sofas at the opposite end of the giant studio for their respective interviews and end-of-show banter.

Willard Scott's weather map was an actual map with temperatures, clouds, and weather fronts applied by hand long before I found my spot near the dark edge of the main set. Willard was the loud, fun uncle behind the scenes that he portrayed on air. Gene Shalit, the legendary movie critic with the bushy black hair and bushy black mustache, taught me a vital life skill: how to tie a bow tie. I knocked on the door of Gene's dimly lit office and asked if I could bother him. I told him I was having trouble figuring out how to tie one. Gene leapt from his cluttered desk, opened the doors of his armoire, pulled out two bow ties, and like a general leading troops into battle, thundered, "Follow me!"

Standing side by side in front of the mirror in the bathroom, Gene patiently demonstrated what to do with the silk around our necks. On the penultimate step, when you have to push the folded loop through the hole created by your thumb to complete the bow tie, I can still hear his voice commanding, "Now, jam it in there!" The last step was straightening up the bow tie, making it look neat. But Gene advised against making it look *too* neat. "Leaving it a little messy," he said, "lets people know you tied it yourself."

Interns were told to walk the rows of cubicles and ask researchers, producers, anyone if they needed help with anything. Because interns come and go, our intelligence, skills, and reliability were always suspect. We had to prove ourselves, and those sitting in judgment were tough. I never said no to an assignment and understood that there was no such thing as a menial task. I called congressional offices and chased down books, music records, VHS tapes of movies, and the latest-issue magazines. I sent broadcast tapes and other materials by way of "the pouch," a magical bag that somehow made its way from 30 Rock to NBC News bureaus around the world. And I used a new technology called "rapifax." I didn't just mindlessly photocopy the stacks of newspaper and magazine articles and various research notes I was given. I read them to learn what the researcher or producer was working on, which helped me understand the importance of anticipating problems. I asked lots of questions.

And I made plenty of mistakes. My journals from those internship summers are filled with many examples. Like the time at the end of the day, when a show researcher asked me to gather information on drought, farmers, President Reagan, and Richard Lyng, his secretary of agriculture. I got all of it but took it home to sort out and give to her the next day. Watching *Today* that morning, I realized the huge error I'd made. Secretary Lyng was a guest on the show. The stoicism of the researcher in response to my apology barely masked her irritation. Another time, a researcher on location in London asked me to send two tapes she needed for a story on Wimbledon. It wasn't until her return that I learned she never got them and had to get the footage from the BBC. Turned out the guy in the mailroom never sent her the flight information needed to get the tapes. Both were lessons in follow-through and paying attention to detail that guide me to this day. Not only did I learn the importance of owning up to my professional mishaps, but I also learned the importance of doing better going forward.

Those journals show that I didn't know what I didn't know about news, journalism, and even life. They show how I loved every minute of learning how to fill in those gaps. And they hold a grounding piece of advice that legendary television journalist Linda Ellerbee left with her autograph days after the news broke that she was leaving the *Today* show: "<u>Remember</u>—it's <u>only</u> television." By underlining "remember" once and "only" twice, Ellerbee gave me a golden rule that I wouldn't fully appreciate until I had a television show of my own.

Early in my first internship in 1986, I worked on the show that was broadcast live from Governors Island on July Fourth in celebration of the one hundredth birthday of the Statue of Liberty. In the predawn hours, I made my way to Lower Manhattan to catch the ferry and somehow found myself sitting with Maria Shriver and some of her siblings for the short ride over. The niece and nephew of the late president John F. Kennedy were talking about trying to visit the aircraft carrier named for him anchored in New York Harbor for the festivities. Upon arrival at the *Today* show location, I was given green room duty. That is, tending to the needs of the show's guests and escorting them from the holding area to the raised set that had as a backdrop the majestic view of the Lady in the Harbor.

The most memorable guests that morning for me were Senator Bob Dole, then the Senate Republican Conference chair, and his wife, Elizabeth, then the secretary of transportation. Rumors were swirling that the senior senator from Kansas was going to run for president in 1988. Standing side by side off camera, waiting to move them into place, I leaned into the World War II veteran and whispered, "Are you going to run for president?" He bent his head sideways in my direction and whispered, "Yeah, are you going to help me?" I squealed, "Yes!" But by the time of the Minnesota caucuses in 1988, I was one of the lonely few standing in support of bow-tie-clad Illinois Senator Paul Simon.

Later in the evening of July Fourth, I left college friends in the crush of Lower Manhattan and used my NBC credentials in the vain hope of getting back on Governors Island for a spectacular view of the fireworks. Donning my NBC News hat, I hopped over a concrete barricade and ran down empty streets cordoned off by the police, to whom I name-dropped NBC three times by the time I got to the ferry terminal. "No ferries will be running until 11 p.m.," an officer told me at the entrance. I decided to wait inside the ferry terminal where then–New York prosecutor Rudy Giuliani was also trying to get to Governors Island. Within minutes, they locked the doors and ushered us onto a ferry, which pushed out of the sleeve far enough for us to see the Statue of Liberty and the spectacular fireworks that burst over our heads.

I worked with so many wonderful people at NBC News those two summers. Mary Alice O'Rourke was the den mother of the interns, in addition to being a writer on the show. Cheryl Wells, Ronee Hoade, Rosemarie Barone, Katherine Perry, Janice "J.J." DeRosa, Marianne Hagerty were just some of the great people I got to work with and learn from. Andre Poulin was a researcher, and as the first out gay man I ever worked with, he was a superb role model. Even when he was stressed out, he radiated warmth and joy.

As the *After 8* producer, Cindy Samuels was deep into national politics. From interactions on the show and on the campaign trail, she had great stories and insights into the politicians she covered. Cindy was also very cool. With curly blond hair and a tiny red-lipstick-covered mouth, Cindy looked like Bernadette Peters and had the same bubbly personality. She not only took me under her wing, but also unwittingly turned me into a New Yorker.

For the month of August 1987 and again in 1988, Cindy and her husband asked me to house-sit and take care of the family's cute, elderly dog. They lived in the Apthorp, a grand prewar building that was the setting for Nora Ephron's book *Heartburn* and the 1986 movie adaptation. My buddy Anthony Sozio, who worked at the *Today* show front desk and was the gregarious son of an NBC News cameraman, stayed with me. We dubbed our summer digs "The Palace." One weekend during the summer of 1987, we hosted a few of my college classmates for "Capehart-o-Rama," a fun weekend of showing them around the city I swore I'd live in one day.

Steve Friedman, the legendary executive producer who took the show to No. 1 and kept it there for years, was always willing to answer questions and dispense advice. For instance, he told me not to bother with journalism graduate school because it was better to learn by doing. When I asked him to look at the rundown for the news show I was developing for the college radio station, he said bluntly, "People watch people, not rundowns. Report things people won't hear anywhere else." And when I asked him to sign my journal, he wrote, "Give me a job one day." More than two decades later, as executive producer of *The Cycle*,

MSNBC's version of *The View*, Steve put me into the rotation of guest hosts when one of the regulars was away.

Steve was close to perhaps the most consequential person I worked with. A trash-talking Mets fanatic whose manner reminded me so much of my mother's brothers, the ones who jabbed me in the arm and tried to box with me to toughen me up. That political producer was and remains a guy's guy. I was and remain not that kind of guy. As a result, I found Phil Griffin terrifying. And yet we clicked.

Phil was like a demanding five-star general of a television news boot camp. The words "I can't" were not acceptable. I fielded his every phone call, made calls for him, hunted down the tapes he requested, and made sure they were all in the overnight pouch or FedEx package headed his way. When Phil changed plans and dumped the Cross State Iowa Bike Race in Des Moines in favor of going to Omaha, Nebraska, I had to find him a bicycle there. He also had me call the Muscatine, Iowa, city hall to ask where the prettiest spot in town was. Once, when he called his desk from London and another intern answered his phone, he had another producer tell me to camp out at his desk because he didn't want anyone else sitting there.

I was nineteen years old when I met Phil. On the last day of my summer internship in 1986, he told Steve Friedman he should hire me. In 2009, the year after he was appointed president of MSNBC, Phil was the one who hired me as an on-air contributor. I was forty-one years old. Twelve years later, as I sat in a hotel room high above Manhattan, getting ready to anchor the next morning, Phil called me with news I had dreamed of hearing since before we met. I was getting my own show on MSNBC on Sunday mornings.

One of the enduring memories of the 1987 internship was sitting on the "working set" of *NBC Nightly News*. Gay Pirozzi, a producer on the show, was the one who helped make that happen. Garrick Utley was sitting in for Tom Brokaw. I sat over his left shoulder, and in an effort to look like I was actually doing work, I repeatedly filled my computer screen with "The United States is the greatest nation on earth" because it was something I could type really fast. The lights, the theme music, the action all around was exciting and I was in the middle of it. A bit player in an important enterprise.

In the last two weeks of my internship, I was hired as a temporary employee by NBC and worked in the "Special Segment" unit. I answered phones, xeroxed, and messengered or delivered tapes for the team, which included Garrick Utley. Also on the team was a warm, handsome, stylish, and married-with-children producer named Joe DeCola, who made twenty-year-old me tingle. Ann Rubenstein was also part of that team. She and I met the previous summer when she came from Chicago to sit in for Jane one week. I asked her then if I could talk to her about the news business one day. She replied, "Oh, 'the biz'? Get down, sure no problem...Whenever you want." Ann has been a friend and mentor giving me advice about "the biz" and life ever since.

I also learned from some stellar Black journalists. Allison Davis was the show's set writer-producer, an important position that put the anchors in her hands if there was breaking news or last-minute changes during the show. With Bryant, there were always changes and Allison knew how to write in "Gumbel-ese," she told me. As one of the most senior African Americans working on the show, Allison was a role model. As was Bert Medley, the avuncular producer who was as patient as he was wise. In the

1990s, Bert and Allison were early adopters of the technology that would power the forthcoming digital revolution. In fact, Allison is the person Katie Couric famously asked, "Allison, can you explain what Internet is?" Together, Bert and Allison were the power behind NBC's partnership with Microsoft and the later formation of MSNBC.com. I worked even more closely with researchers Adrienne Wheeler and Dotty Anderson. All were great teachers, imparting implicit and explicit lessons on what it means to be Black in the news business. But the best role model on that score was the one who inspired me to want to be in "the biz" the most: Bryant.

At the end of the first internship in September 1986, I got what would be a consequential assignment from Trish Peters, Bryant's assistant, who looked like Teri Garr and shared the actress's warm and funny personality. She knew Bryant was my idol, primarily because I told her multiple times. So I was over-the-moon excited when she asked me to come to her desk because Bryant had a project for me.

Trish's desk sat outside Bryant's office, surrounded by tall file cabinets. The kind with five or six drawers inside. She opened the top drawer of one to reveal hanging folders filled with yellow legal pads, explaining they held interviews Bryant had done for the show. What he wanted, Trish said, was a cover sheet for each legal pad that would include the date, name of the guest, and the subject discussed. Having something he could see at a glance would make it easier for him to hunt down past interviews with repeat guests, such as members of Congress. This task had all the hallmarks of a make-work assignment. There were dozens of interviews per legal pad and an endless supply of them in each file drawer. From the first legal pad to the last, I was in heaven.

What I admired most about Bryant was how he conducted interviews. As I slogged through one legal pad after another, the project took me inside his head. Each page started out neat. He wrote his questions legibly in longhand. But the page also revealed his mind at work during an interview. A change in the order of his neatly composed questions was noted by numbers jotted on the left side. Because I made a point of reading every question, his hasty scribbles and maniacal numbering made more and more sense as I read one interview after another. He reordered his questions in real time. He took notes out of camera range, jotting down words and phrases that he might employ in a later question. Bryant was an active listener, and it came through on camera. It is a skill that I employ when conducting my own interviews. The most important lesson I learned was that Bryant worked hard to be prepared. I saw it in those legal pads, and everyone saw it on television.

On the morning of September 5, 1986, I saw all that I had learned about Bryant in action. Because it was the last day of my first summer internship, I got to the studio before the 7:00 a.m. show went on air. And it promised to be a big day. Tennis great Billie Jean King, legendary actress Helen Hayes, and pop group Bananarama, whose song "Venus" was the anthem of the summer, were due to appear. But news was breaking out of Karachi, Pakistan, that Pan Am Flight 73 had been hijacked.

Mere minutes before air, I watched Bryant scribble down at all angles the information he was getting from the control room as he asked various questions in response to what he was being told. Then, he and guest host Jean Enersen, an anchor from NBC's Seattle affiliate, went live and I watched Bryant distill those hastily scribbled notes into a coherent narration of events unfolding nine hours ahead of New York. It was an impressive display that left me more in awe of him than before and became the template for my anchor style today.

I considered my relationship with Bryant complicated. And I use the word "relationship" loosely. He was my hero. But I often found my hero cold or indifferent toward me. More often than not, he would walk by me like I was an apparition, the Ghost of Annoying Interns Present. So on the first day of my second summer internship, I was prepared for more of the same. As usual, I made it to my in-studio perch in time for the 7:30 a.m. start of the show and stayed glued to that spot until the show was over at 9:00 a.m. I hovered in the shadows off the main set watching all the post-show action. That's when I noticed Bryant making his way to the doors behind me to exit Studio 3B. As he approached, I vowed to myself that I would neither acknowledge nor speak to him. He acted like I didn't exist so it wouldn't matter, I thought. The closer he got, the louder the chatter in my head grew. When he walked right by me without looking, I felt the snub in my soul. But then, without breaking his stride, Bryant popped me on the shoulder and said, "Welcome back!"

That moment taught me a valuable professional lesson. You are not as invisible as you might think or feel. People are always watching. They are taking note. They are rendering judgments about you based on information you don't realize you're providing. And oftentimes, the chatter in your head is the incessant ramblings of your own insecurities.

This extraordinary opportunity all began with the kindness of my Uncle McKinley.

As luck would have it, years later, one of the times I substitute-anchored *Way Too Early* for host Willie Geist coincided with McKinley's impending retirement from NBC in 2012 after forty-one years. Because the show aired live at 5:30 a.m., I was usually sitting in Geist's office by 4:00 a.m. going over scripts, especially the sports scripts. (Lord, nothing was more terrible than me doing sports. But I was like the movie *Showgirls*. I was so bad, I was good. A camp classic.) During those insane hours, McKinley was at work doing the overnight shift and would swing by Willie's office to visit me.

On the last morning of my substitute duty, I asked McKinley what time he got off work. He told me 8:30 a.m. but that he would be leaving closer to 9:00 a.m. Perfect. I would still be on air at that hour with *Morning Joe*. He initially tried to get out of accepting my invitation to come to the *Morning Joe* set, especially after I told him I wanted to give him a send-off during the "What have we learned today?" segment that closed the then-three-hour program. When he arrived on set, hosts Joe Scarborough and Mika Brzezinski enthusiastically agreed to let me bring McKinley on to celebrate his retirement. A live national television audience got to see my bashful uncle smile in a beautiful mix of pride and humility as I explained why his simple kindness of letting me visit him in that building twenty-six years earlier put me on a path that allowed me to honor him on television, a path that launched me into the life I enjoy now. Rewatching that moment years later, I realized I never actually said the words "thank you." A couple of days before McKinley died of cancer in 2020, I got to say just that.

That path McKinley helped put me on began with two steps taken on the very same day. The phone call to him was really the second step. The first was the reason that brought me to Midtown that day in 1985 in the first place: my Carleton College admissions interview. Without a doubt, just about every wonderful thing that has happened in my life can be traced back to my decision to go to that small liberal arts college in Minnesota.

CHAPTER 7

EVERYTHING AROUND ME CAME ALIVE

I first learned about Carleton College from a young Black woman during a student council convention trip to Reno, Nevada, in 1982. The kind where we were placed with families in the area. Mine lived in a nice house whose simple charms were overshadowed by the runway of the nearby military airfield, where jets roared in and out with surround-sound ferocity.

Carol Barnett introduced herself to me at the bottom of the hill, where she stood as a bunch of us came down during a hike. For an incoming freshman to the Minnesota college, Carol had her Carleton sales pitch down cold and advised, "When it's time for you to start looking at colleges, you should keep Carleton in mind." It was the summer after my freshman year in high school so looking at colleges was a ways off. But when the time came, I remembered her enthusiasm about the small liberal arts college in the town that annually reenacts the failed attempt by the Jesse James gang to rob its bank.

The course catalog and a pamphlet with a watercolor of the college's chapel tower captured my imagination once they arrived. I flipped through it so many times, the staples gave up holding the glossy pages in place. But I had questions. So many questions! I called the admissions office every day, several times a day, connecting with Beth Clary. I had the phone number memorized, and if the person who answered didn't sound like Miss Clary, I would ask to speak with her.

How does financial aid work? How long are the classes? How many classes do I have to take? What are the dorms like? What's Northfield like? Why do you have trimesters and not semesters like everyone else? You mean we take off the entire month of December? Because of the cold, there are tunnels that students use to get around some parts of campus? Wait, how cold *does* it get there? For this shy kid, Miss Clary's kind voice, its timbre and the unhurried pace at which she spoke, was an invitation to linger, to go beyond the original purpose of the call, and to phone again. No question was too inane for me to ask or for her to answer.

One day, my mother delivered a warning. She advised me to ease up on the calls lest I become a pest and hurt my chances of getting accepted. I heeded Mom's counsel. The very next day, the phone rang at home. "Hello, Jonathan? This is Beth Clary at Carleton College," she said. Like I didn't know who she was. "I didn't hear from you yesterday," she continued, "so I wanted to make sure everything was all right. Did you have any more questions you wanted answered?" I was momentarily speechless. Not only was Miss Clary calling *me*, she was also giving me permission to *be* me in all my inquisitiveness. My mother told me years later that it was that one phone call that told her everything she needed to know about Carleton. "I knew you'd be going somewhere you'd be nurtured," she told me. "There would be people who cared about you."

First, though, I had to get accepted. I was no child genius, but my grades were good. St. Benedict's was challenging in ways that Raritan High School had not been. I thrived under the academic pressure that came with being a Gray Bee. But I feared the SAT. It was one of those life-and-death tests like the ones that stamped me as having a low IQ. Someone lacking the necessary intelligence for college, let alone an institution like Carleton.

The conventional wisdom then was you should take the SAT twice, especially if you get a score you didn't like. Your second set of SAT scores would be higher than your first. My heart sank when I learned that out of a perfect 1600, my combined score totaled less than 1000. So you can imagine my state of panic when my results came back even lower after taking the SAT a second time. In the decades since I suffered through those exams, experts have slammed the test as being culturally biased in ways detrimental to students of color, particularly African Americans. That wasn't the case for me. Most of my childhood was spent in predominantly white towns going to predominantly white schools. Therefore, my problem wasn't cultural. It was nerves. I simply didn't test well. And I feared those dismal scores would keep me from going to college.

Miss Clary allayed those fears. She assured me that SAT scores were not the only measure Carleton considered for admission. I applied to a wide range of schools, from big schools like Syracuse University with its famed broadcast journalism school, Historically Black Howard University, to Swarthmore College. But my mind and heart were set on Carleton.

If I were to ever give my then-stepfather any credit for anything, it would be his introduction to an old family friend of his. Dr. William M. Chase lived on the other side of Meeker Avenue. He and his wife were frequent visitors, and he took an interest in my college search. When I mentioned Carleton to Dr. Chase, he told me that he had been a member of the board of trustees of the National Medical Association and that the Maryland-based nonprofit that represents the interests of Black physicians gave scholarships to Black students to attend Carleton. Dr. Chase told me that if I got accepted, he'd get me the scholarship. I got both.

My flight to Minneapolis and Carleton freshmen orientation was the biggest moment of my life so far. No words can describe my excitement as I watched Newark disappear and the Twin Cities come into view from my window. I was on a plane whose destination was of my choosing. A place that would mark the beginning of adulthood and the creation of a life of my own. From the airport van, I saw a landscape that was familiar to what I saw during my summers in North Carolina. When we rounded the bend, I saw the Gothic Revival bell tower of Skinner Memorial Chapel standing tall in the sun. And I felt at home.

When you're a Black freshman at Carleton, you also meet your peer counselor, a Black upperclassman who is meant to make your transition to rural Northfield smoother. This reflected Carleton's long history of not only recruiting Black students, but also doing everything possible to keep them. In 1964, the college received a landmark grant from the Rockefeller Foundation to enroll students of color, African Americans in particular.

Getting used to Carleton and Northfield wasn't a problem. I loved it there. The campus was green in the spring and summer. A blaze of yellows, browns, and reds in the fall. And a wind tunnel for the frigid wind that raced in from the west, carrying the burning smell of the Malt-O-Meal cereal plant a mile away. Being in this overwhelmingly white environment didn't concern me at all—until I needed to get a haircut. Things were fine as long as the Black upperclassman with the clippers my peer counselor told me about was able to buzz me down to my usual little-boy-bald look. But then they broke. Waiting for them to get repaired wasn't going to be a big deal. The temporary solution was called a pack-down, where you pack down your damp hair by wearing a stocking cap overnight. When you have nappy hair like mine, it does the trick. In the morning, the tightly coiled hair looks like a coarse helmet.

But as the days passed, my crunchy Afro felt uncomfortable and made me self-conscious. I looked like a mess. My erstwhile barber with the good hair and broken clippers told me to go to his barber. A white man in town. Of course, his barber would know how to handle his hair. But mine?

Bridge Square Barber in downtown Northfield had been owned by David Downhour since 1969, the quintessential Midwestern man with a quiet demeanor and friendly face. When I walked my unruly mane into the joint in the mid-1980s, I found him standing by the chair talking to two friends. I asked for a haircut. He welcomed me to have a seat.

What happened next was comically awkward. As Mr. Downhour stood behind me, he repeatedly said "Oh!" with a distinctly

Minnesotan inflection as his hands hovered over my head, undecided about what to do. "I've never cut your type of hair before," he said. I told him it was easy. All he needed were hair clippers. Growing up, my haircuts took all of five minutes. Like an army recruit reporting for basic training. Zip, zip, zip. All done. He was too afraid to use them. He used his scissors instead.

Mr. Downhour required more reassurance as he went about his task. I told him that I had so much hair that if he made a mistake, there was plenty of room to recover. That was me being hopeful. The night before class pictures in the seventh and eighth grades, Mom gave me the same assurance after putting a blowout kit in my hair and then cutting the newly straightened mop. Each time, she sent me butchered before the cameras. So all I could do was pray that a professional like Mr. Downhour would get it right, despite the challenge he faced with my wooly hair.

The longer he took, the more I settled into anxious resignation. Anxious for him to finish. Resigned to the disaster surely to come at the hands of this white man, once he handed me the mirror. I gasped when Mr. Downhour had me take a look. I wanted to cry. It was the best haircut I'd ever had. He cut my hair for the rest of my time at Carleton.

There weren't that many Black students on campus my freshman year. The fact that I didn't go out of my way to hang out with many of them bothered my peer counselor so much that he pulled me outside of an event to raise his concern. He couldn't understand why I was not more part of "the community." I was kind of amused that his concern was how well I fit in. The predominantly white environment was neither foreign nor intimidating to me.

For me, Carleton was a return to a comfort zone. A rigorous academic environment surrounded by white students who were not unlike the ones I grew up with in New Jersey. But I also understood that the experience was not universally shared in the reverse. The closest some of my classmates probably came to knowing a Black person was on NBC on Thursday nights when the Huxtables of Brooklyn Heights beamed Black excellence into their homes. I was a real Black person they could get to know, and I relished getting to know them.

My freshman dorm room was on the third floor of Myers Hall, a brown brick shoe box on the eastern edge of campus. My roommate was Tim Kirker, a great guy from Maine who was an expert on Steely Dan, Donald Fagen and his debut album *The Nightfly.* Tim also brought with him loads of clothes from L.L.Bean, which he let me wear. If what he wanted to wear wasn't in his closet, he was sure to find it in mine.

Tim and I spent countless hours playing the card game hearts with Paul and John on the other side of the hall. Paul and Tim could usually be seen with a lump of chewing tobacco under their bottom lip. Tim, Paul, and John were butch guys. The kind of guys who didn't fuss over their appearance like the fourth wheel hunched around the makeshift card table.

Heeding the advice I received during my *Today* show internships, I majored in political science and took as many history classes as I could. The study of political science and history is one of cold, hard facts. This happened on this date for this or that reason and here were the consequences of said action or actions. After three years of classes in that style of instruction, at first my brain could not handle the squishiness of an art history class I had signed up for my senior year. Everything was open to interpretation. But then a light switch went off—literally.

Professor Alison Kettering had a captivating way of lecturing. Her instruction always started slowly, her soft voice guiding us through the paintings or sculptures displayed on the screen. As the lesson went on, her pace increased. The urgency built during her lecture as she tied seemingly disparate ideas into a coherent and mind-blowing lesson, hitting the last word of her talk like a soprano reaching an aria-ending high-C. And after a beat, a click of the light switch. That moment—the lesson, the performance of that lesson, the theater of it all—hooked me.

Professor Kettering helped me to see a world of beauty in things all around me, and everything came alive. I started looking at pictures with an eye for composition and light, for what is seen and not seen in the frame. I saw architecture where I had once simply seen buildings. How many times had I looked out that bathroom window in Newark and not even really noticed the Basilica of the Sacred Heart in the distance? During my senior winter break, I raced across town to see the Gothic architecture that made Chartres and Notre Dame famous, replicated on a grand church in my own backyard.

Another unforeseen passion found during college was ballroom dancing, something I discovered while looking for a way to fulfill the physical education requirement that didn't involve taking off my clothes in a locker room filled with other men. I'd always loved dancing. The R & B, disco, and soul music of my childhood demanded it. To not move while "Ain't No Stopping Us Now" is playing is a crime against the race. Soon, I was tearing up the dance floor in the Cowling Gymnasium with Sara, a native of Gainesville, Florida, who had lived in my dorm freshman year and loved the glamour of old movies like *Breakfast at Tiffany's*. Ignoring the instructor's command to change partners, Sara and I mastered the foxtrot, waltz, polka, and Lindy Hop. For years, we were a team. So it made sense that I would ask her to be my girlfriend. It also made sense that she said no. Not out of any lack of love. We were great friends, and it was our friendship she wanted to preserve. And perhaps my motive for making such an ask was transparent. The ask was my last-ditch effort to be straight.

All in all, I was a mediocre student in college. I loved going to class, but my grades never matched my enthusiasm. If anything, they reflected my enthusiasm for what I was doing outside of the classroom. That is, being a journalist, which kicked into high gear in the winter term of my junior year when I was the news editor of the *Carletonian*, the school newspaper, and news director of KRLX, the campus radio station. The paper was in a room at the top of Sayles-Hill Campus Center. I spent many a night there running printed copy through the glue machine and then laying out the lines of text on the page for final printing. That was before my classmate Becky Loraas fired me after I helped start a rival one-sheet publication called the *COW*, the *Carleton Observer Weekly*, which scooped the *Carletonian* by publishing the night before. She was right.

The radio station was in the basement of Sayles-Hill, a time capsule filled with vinyl records and a teletype machine rushing in news from United Press International. With all the local, state, and national news I gathered and the PSAs to break up the content, I would walk into the studio, put on the headphones, adjust the levels, and get to work. The theme music for *KRLX News at Six* was the urgent opening instrumental of Gloria Estefan's "Rhythm Is Going to Get You." How very

1980s. Sir Edward Elgar's Pomp and Circumstance March No. 4 in G Major, the music for my Sunday affairs show called *Sunday Review*, was not.

My GPA might have suffered, but my personal satisfaction was off the charts. I couldn't wait to get out into the real world and do it all for a living. Harry Goldstein, a hyper and brilliant guy from Louisville, Kentucky, reminiscent of a young Dustin Hoffman, was my journalism soul mate. He was Carl Bernstein to my Bob Woodward. He smoked clove cigarettes and listened to jazz. His favorite album, *Francis Albert Sinatra & Antônio Carlos Jobim*, became the soundtrack of my junior year and remains one of my favorite albums today. I loved chasing stories on campus for the newspaper. Honing my skills. Learning to be observant, to notice patterns and how changes in these patterns could be the result of news. Most importantly, I learned to listen. I relished the knowledge that would come from another person, their expertise, their opinion, their experience. And I put that curiosity to the test my sophomore year with a full-front-page story that had as its graphic a cinder block wall with what looked like spray-painted words that served as the headline: "Homosexuals at Carleton."

If college is a journey of self-discovery, then mine began in earnest earlier that year upon meeting Matthew Brooks. He was a freshman from Santa Fe, New Mexico, whose good looks and five o'clock shadow pegged him as a doppelgänger of the singer George Michael. He was gay. He didn't lead with it. He didn't hide it. It was inherently who he was. His eyes, smile, and deep dimples all conspired to make you fall in love with him. That's what happened to anyone who met Matthew. That's what happened to me.

We lived on the same floor of Goodhue Hall, an out-of-the-way residential hall on the eastern edge of campus. From the moment we met, we were inseparable. We both loved classical music. He introduced me to Mahler's Symphony No. 5, which led me to Shostakovich's Symphony No. 5 and Prokofiev's Symphony No. 5, Bombastic works that I still listen to, especially when I'm writing. Matthew played piano beautifully and rehearsed all the time. In the winter of 1987, I sat next to him on a piano bench in the Music Hall and came out.

Matthew wasn't the only gay person on campus. But he was the one I most wanted to be like. He was comfortable in his own skin more than a decade before *Will & Grace* taught America they had Matthews in their lives, if they'd only see and accept them. He had a quiet swagger about him as he walked around campus in cowboy boots and a leather jacket. He was gracious and charming. He became my best friend. My first conversation in the morning. My last conversation at night. We spent so much time together that we could finish each other's sentences. Better still, we could sit with each other, say nary a word, and still have a full conversation in the silence. He made me want to be better as a person, do better. Ours was never a romantic relationship. It was a deeply emotional one, a friendship where I felt genuine love for him and from him. A bond that remains today. Even when he started dating Mark, an upperclassman who was the epitome of the sexy nerd, our friendship didn't change. Mark became a good friend of mine, too.

The confidence and leadership Matthew exhibited while being his true self made him a role model for me and others on campus. He moved the meetings of what was called the LGBC—Lesbian, Gay, Bisexual at Carleton—from the basement of the chapel to a big meeting room on the second floor of Sayles-Hill. The hiddenness of the former location perpetuated shame. The openness of the latter location connoted self-respect and pride. At a time when folks were hiding they were gay, Matthew spent his junior year increasing the LGBC's visibility, including going to every dorm during freshman orientation week to talk about the group and what it did. As a result, anyone who came out at Carleton between 1988 and 1990 most likely talked to Matthew first. Carleton was not without its problems. When someone scrawled "fag" on a painting of Matthew's in an art studio classroom his junior year, he organized a campus-wide vigil that was backed by college president Steve Lewis. It was a turning point for the LGBC community.

It took me a while to follow his example, even after coming out to him. I was more than happy to hide behind his leadership and confidence, to let people draw their own conclusions about me because of our friendship. But my hiding in plain sight was akin to ducking behind a sapling in the middle of an open field. "Homosexuals at Carleton" was my initial way of trying to understand who I was. I wasn't an opinion writer then. I was a dispassionate news reporter. Asking questions. Getting answers. And consequently, learning about myself. I spent three weeks talking with twelve gay men and six lesbians about life on campus. I changed their names to protect their privacy. Matthew was one of them. Contrary to what I learned some people thought at the time, I was not. But I did see myself reflected in their words and their stories. I saw with more clarity that I wasn't alone.

I certainly had Black friends at Carleton, but by my junior year, the scant number of African Americans spiked. There were so many new faces on campus, I quipped excitedly to another,

"Where'd all these Black people come from?" The Black students of the incoming class of 1991 were smart and lively, and very active in campus life. That incoming class contributed to discourse on race and politics by being loud voices for Carleton to divest from South Africa and increased diversity at the college. And because some of them were members of the LGBC, they helped make the group an even more visible part of campus life. My two identities were in harmony.

My dreams of getting a job at the *Today* show after graduation disappeared as the impact of General Electric's purchase of RCA, the parent company of NBC, three years earlier became manifest. The people who could hire me were gone or afraid for their own jobs. Meanwhile, my hunt for jobs at the Minneapolis affiliates went nowhere and I spectacularly bombed an interview with WCVB in Boston. Thankfully, I found a job. Every year, Carleton gave a year-long fellowship to a graduating senior to serve as assistant to the president the following academic year. For 1989–90, that person was me. But what was supposedly a Plan B turned out to be the best plan of all.

CHAPTER 8

HIDE YOUR PORN WELL!

The message on the answering machine was not unexpected. Ricardo told me he would call. It was the tone that caught my attention. Sounding subdued, my junior-year college roommate told me he'd returned from the house in Newark, and to give him a call back. Panic filled me as I stood in the darkened living room of my apartment in Nourse Hall, where I was the head resident during my 1989–90 tenure as assistant to the president of Carleton.

Since my sophomore year, I had been out. First to Matthew, my best friend, and then to others as the college years rolled on. Long before I sat down on that piano bench or wrote "Homosexuals at Carleton," I knew I was gay—basically, since I was ten years old. I didn't have words for my feelings until I read about men lying with men in some Bible tract in the bathroom at my Uncle Johnnie's house when I was thirteen. Something about seeing those words, the recognition they stirred, inspired relief. The language of abomination and sin that followed left no doubt that my newfound sexual orientation was considered a moral malady. Not a surprise since "faggot" and "*maricón*," the Spanish version of the slur, floated in the air and the culture like glitter. As hard as you tried to avoid it, you couldn't help coming into contact with it. Now, many years later, not yet having the courage to come out to my mother and stepfather, I stood frozen in fear, as if a circus clown were about to hit me in the face with handfuls of that glitter.

I don't remember how Ricardo, the son of Cuban immigrants from Teaneck, and I met. But as Jersey gay boys, a shared goal of leading the glamorous life in Manhattan after college was what sealed our bond. His move back home after graduation made it possible for him to make the twenty-mile drive to the house on Meeker Avenue to complete the urgent mission I assigned him.

Ricardo had to rescue my porn stash.

I kept the cache of erotica in the eaves, which you accessed through a mint-green door that required a butter knife to open. That's where my stepfather once stored things he no longer had use for. Rooting around in there when we moved in six years earlier, I found an incredible collection of pornographic magazines. *Playboy, Penthouse, Penthouse Forum, Hustler.* A goldmine for a hormonal teenage boy. A collection that acquired new titles like *Honcho, Playguy, Inches,* and *Advocate Men* as I tried to figure out who and what I liked. The Gucci box that once held the tennis racket cover Aunt Elsie bought me for my birthday a few years back was now the repository for my blinding material. The near-daily use of my hidden library took its toll on the box, though. The once sturdy cardboard had grown brittle and yawned under its increasing weight. Removing it from the eaves during breaks from Carleton required great care. When I dispatched Ricardo to retrieve it, I urged him to bring tape, lest it fall apart in his hands.

Ricardo's urgent mission was necessary because the day before, Mom called to tell me that her marriage to my stepfather was on the verge of collapse. She didn't know how much longer she would be with him, but the time of her departure was drawing near. After coordinating with Ricardo, I called Mom to let her know that he would be stopping by to pick something up that I needed back at Carleton before she hightailed it out of there. And Ricardo was to call me once the mission was accomplished.

"Hey, Ricardo! It's Jonathan," I said excitedly as he answered the phone. Before I could say another word, he asked somberly, "Has your mom called you yet?" My legs went weak as my heart jumped into my mouth. "No!" I said, gasping. "Why? What happened?!"

Ricardo said that both my mom and stepfather were there when he arrived. The trio talked for a few minutes and then Ricardo said he should probably get up to my room and get going. My mom followed him up the stairs, chattering away, asking if he needed any help. "No. I know where it is," Ricardo told her as he left her on the second floor to ascend to my room. "Jonathan told me exactly where to find it."

As instructed, he used the butter knife that sat atop the molding around the small door to pull it open. Ricardo said he quickly wrapped the box up in the tape he brought with him and eased it out of the eaves. "You find everything okay?" my mom asked as he came down the stairs. "Yes, Mrs. Hunt," he said, using her married name. He moved quickly down the stairs because he wasn't sure how long the tape would securely hold my sizable collection.

Each detail in Ricardo's unspooling story filled me with dread. I just knew it was going to end horribly. Ricardo then said that as he rounded the last bend of the stairs to get to the first floor, he tripped. "The box flew out of my hand and disintegrated when it hit the floor," he said. "They went everywhere." My life flashed before my eyes as I screamed, "What?! What?! Oh my God! What?!"

I imagined a scene of glossy pages of erections and depictions of unspeakable acts I once enjoyed under cover of darkness splayed out on the hunter green carpet at the bottom of the stairs. Of my newly born-again Christian mother standing aghast amid the mess. Of my stepfather chuckling at the confirmation of what he'd always known. After all, he was the one who had once confronted me about my sexuality by flatly stating, "You know you're a homosexual."

"I grabbed them all as fast as I could and got the hell out of there," Ricardo said as I sat agape in silence more than a thousand miles away. How on earth was I going to explain this? Coming out is a journey. One that must be done at one's own pace and in one's own time. At least, that's what I would come to know years later. But at that moment, I wasn't ready to come out to my family, and I certainly was not ready to talk about something so personal and intimate after something so personal and intimate—and pornographic—had literally landed at their feet. It took time for me to learn that coming out of the closet, declaring one's sexuality, was an empowering and necessary constant.

Early in my newspaper career while writing editorials at the *New York Daily News* about unsafe sex in gay movie theaters, I felt I had no choice but to finally come out to my editor. He couldn't understand why younger gay men were not heeding the lessons learned from older gay men reeling from the ongoing AIDS epidemic. Only by coming out could I answer his queries, and it led me to write a first-person account of my two-and-a-half-hour visit to a gay bathhouse, where I observed: "The sound of water in the shower room draws men like a dinner bell on a dude ranch." But your voice and perspective don't count, you don't exist, if people don't know you're there. This makes coming out inherently political, as well as terrifying.

The silence on the phone that was filled by the cacophony of my thoughts was drowned out by Ricardo's distinctive room-filling laughter. "Everything's fine," he said. "The box is fine."

Mom's tumultuous six-year marriage fell apart a week or so after Ricardo's visit. A furrier in Newark was going out of business, and Mom took advantage of the sale and put a coat on layaway. The store called the house to let her know that her name had been emroidered inside the lining and that the coat, which Grandma later called "the troublemaker," was ready for pickup. Mom wasn't sure if my stepfather took the call or if there had been a message on the answering machine, but he called her at work with the furrier's message and a frightening one of his own: "You better not come back to this house alone."

Heeding the advice of a security guard at the hospital where she worked, Mom called the police and had them meet her and two of her coworkers at the house on Meeker Avenue. She was waiting a block away when she saw one of her husband's friends heading to the house. He asked what she was doing there, and thinking this person was also her friend, she told him she was waiting for the police. Surely, this "friend" tipped off her husband about what was to come because when she arrived with the police, he opened the door and said, "Come on in!" He carried on as she packed up her Porsche car, including the plastic bag into which he had raked all her cosmetics, lotions, and potions from the bathroom counter. After she left, she called Aunt Annie to tell her what happened. Annie told her to come to their place in the Bronx.

When I moved back East after Carleton, I spent almost two weeks sleeping on one part of the sectional sofa in the living room with my cousin Justin on another part. My mom had taken up residence in his room upon her arrival three months earlier. She couldn't move back to Hazlet because the tenants to whom she rented the condo were still there. This was not the return to the East Coast that I imagined. I was back from Minnesota, new job in hand. Mayor David Dinkins, the newly elected and first Black mayor of New York City, had appointed Tom Morgan, a Carleton trustee, to be the next president of WNYC, the radio and television stations then owned by the city. He was looking for an administrative assistant for public affairs. Tom tried to scare me a bit by repeatedly describing the job as "low pay, long hours, and lots of grief." I gladly accepted.

And yet, as I sat on the concrete terrace watching planes glide down over the Bronx on their final approach to LaGuardia, even the infectious dance song of the summer, "Everybody, Everybody" by Black Box, wasn't enough to push aside my sadness. When I was growing up, one of Mom's mantras was "Don't be dependent on anyone for anything. You have to learn to be self-sufficient." That was why she taught me how to boil water for pasta, scramble eggs, bake chicken, do laundry, iron my clothes, get from point A to point B. That mindset drives me today. This was also a necessity. Mom often worked extra shifts at the hospital for overtime pay. And in a quest to advance her career and salary, she went to then Kean College at night to get her bachelor's in special ed and a master's in audiology and communications. But here we were imposing on family in their small apartment. Our lives were in upheaval. The highfalutin view Mom and I had of ourselves smacked head-long into reality.

When the divorce became final, Mom had to get the rest of our things out of the house in Newark within two weeks. The day we drove over was the same day Mom and I could move back to Hazlet. Many times during their marriage, my stepfather pressured Mom to sell her condo so they could buy another one in Cape May. Even going so far as to have a Realtor call her. Each time, she refused.

On moving day, my mother's oldest brother was behind the wheel of the van. His twin sons, my cousins, came along to help, too. All of us were ready for a long, depressing moving day. Not only would we have to go to the house in Newark, but we would also have to deal with my stepfather, who was not above hectoring antagonists. So many things to pack up or throw away. So many memories to contend with as Mom and I stripped our presence from his house. What a malevolent presence he was. Like a tasteless, odorless gas that quietly extinguishes life from the unsuspecting. I dreaded seeing him and I ached for my mother. What indignities might he put her through this final time in front of us all?

My stepfather met us in the driveway. He made it clear that we would not be entering the house. Instead, he clicked the garage door opener. As the door slowly rolled up, our possessions came into view. I can't speak for anyone else, but a mixture of relief and disbelief washed over me. Relief because we were saved from the toil of packing, racing up and down stairs, squeezing past each other with arms filled with boxes. All under his overseer's eye. Disbelief, because my stepfather had kicked Mom out of the house—again. Given his facility for meanness, I suppose we should have been grateful that he didn't kick us and our things literally to the curb, like that time he threw Mom's clothes on the front lawn in one of his bully boy tantrums.

Mom said when she walked back into our empty Hazlet home, she finally felt at peace. As would I a few days later when, back in my old room, I finally came out to my mother. It began with an argument. Mom had gone full born-again Christian during her marriage to my stepfather. The Bible became her safe harbor from a union that never should have happened. And now she'd come up to my room to tell me how much of a jerk I'd been since returning from Carleton. She didn't like me calling her out on some of the less-than-kind comments and broad generalizations she'd been making about various folks. "Ever since you came back from Carleton, you haven't been the same. You're not the same child I sent to college," she said. "You've come back from college so, so liberal." She paused after each "so" and practically spit out the word "liberal."

This got me monologuing about oppressed peoples, like a superhero thundering against injustice before putting an end to it. And then I decided to just go there, to create the conditions that would force her to ask the question. In my defense of gays and lesbians, I complained about how they were always talking about getting into the mainstream. "Sometimes I just want to scream, 'Hey! You're already in the mainstream,'" I told her. "'You're doctors, lawyers, judges, journalists. You're everywhere!'" Then came the query whose answer I spent years hiding from her.

"Well, are you gay?"

Sitting on that futon with my legs pretzeled in front of me, I felt exposed, like I was under a spotlight during the final scene of a one-man show. So many times I'd arrived at this point, my moment of truth, and chickened out. I never feared that Mom would kick me out or disown me. Still, I hadn't been ready then to stop crafting and sputtering the lies that reinforce the closet. But that day in my childhood bedroom, with a big gulp and a deep breath, I said, "Yes."

Mom let out a gasp and asked "Why?!" as her hands shot up to her cheeks. I told her that I didn't know why but that I'd known the fact of it since I was ten. Sensing she might go down that route so many parents do to pinpoint the reason for their child's homosexuality, I added, "It's not your fault."

"Fault" wasn't the right word. Mom didn't need my absolution because there was nothing wrong with me, and I didn't feel there was anything wrong with me. Nothing "turned me" gay. I was born gay. People who insist otherwise or who force LGBTQ+ people to deny who they are or even forcibly change who they are through conversion "therapy" are beyond deplorable. For her part, Mom acknowledged there was nothing she could do to change me. The only thing she said she could do was pray for me. And then she wasted no time asking some direct questions.

"Have you had, have you had?" Mom stammered before making hand motions to indicate anal sex. "NO!" I said, to which she replied, "Thank God." She then asked about oral sex and I screamed, "MOTHER!" Yet she persisted. I gave in and said, "Yes." She then asked, "Do you use a condom?" I lied, "Yes." After asking if I had a boyfriend—no, I did not—Mom did a gay roll call as she inquired about each of my friends she'd met.

Then she made three requests: First, "Don't tell anyone else." She worried my coming out would have an impact on career opportunities. My mindset then could be described as "Don't tell, don't deny." I wasn't going to run around telling everyone, but I wasn't going to deny it if someone asked me. How could I? I was gay to the naked eye. Anyone paying attention could see that the only thing straight about me was the crease in my pants. Second, "Don't walk like one." Her demonstration was what we in the Black community call "switchin'," where you exaggeratedly swivel your hips from side to side with every step. In terms of stereotypical gay markers, "switchin'" ranks up there with the limp wrist. When I asked her if I "walked like one," she said no. Third, "Don't go over to any of those marches over there in New York."

Mom apologized when I told her that each of her requests was homophobic. Today, my mother is an embodiment of how far Americans have come in their acceptance of LGBTQ+ people. When Nick and I got married, she said that she now has two sons.

Once I did it, I spent the entire next day giggling. The closet is exhausting. All the little lies you craft, and then tell, and then try to remember to keep your secret require a lot of energy. Like telling my mom that Ricardo and I went dancing at the Palladium, when we were really dancing to disco in the basement of the Monster on Christopher Street. Or that I stayed late in the city to see a movie with friends when I was really at Uncle Charlie's on Greenwich Avenue, hoping a nice-looking man would find this ugly duckling with damaged front teeth, one chipped, the other discolored, attractive enough to talk to. Being liberated from lying gave me reason to smile. All that energy once used to conjure up those lies now had nowhere to go. All I could do was giggle, a silly, contented giggle.

Being back home with Mom seemed like the old days when it was just the two of us. But so much had changed in the six years since we lived there. Mom was divorced and born-again, working a television camera during the Sunday service at the megachurch she attended. I was a college graduate and newly out of the closet. Wondering how long it would take for me to move to the city to start a life of my own. Living back under Mom's roof as an adult was a rough adjustment. I was still her baby, but I was also a grown man with a mind and plans of my own.

Living under Mom's roof also meant sharing a morning drive up to Newark, where she worked and where I commuted to my job at WNYC. As with the drives Down South, there was no time for dillydallying. I had to be showered, dressed, and ready to go no later than 6:30 a.m. Mom would drop me off at Newark Penn Station. I took the PATH train into lower Manhattan to its station under the World Trade Center. I exited aboveground at 5 World Trade Center.

From there, I walked to WNYC's studio and offices inside the Municipal Building now renamed for the late Mayor

Dinkins. My route took me across Vesey Street to Broadway and then along the east side of City Hall Park. So many things caught my eye along the way. The Brooklyn Bridge to my right that teemed with cars spilling into Manhattan from its roadway. In the near distance loomed the Beaux Art grandeur of the Surrogate's Courthouse, where a small eagle stands perched above the sculpted drama of cherubs, City Fathers, and Corinthian columns splayed out beneath it. And then there was the tall, thin, sexy bearded Dutchman named Martin, from whom I bought a blueberry muffin nearly every Wednesday morning. Later, I would go on a date with Martin the Muffin Man and discover that he was a good kisser and possessed a prodigious phallus that I likened to friends as a curved slot machine handle.

Tom's office was inside the Municipal Building's tower, and my desk was within eye-shot of his door and next to floor-to-ceiling windows that faced west, affording me a sweeping view of the Twin Towers, lower Manhattan, and New Jersey spread out in the distance.

For the commute back home, I'd either take the PATH back to Newark and then ride NJ Transit's North Jersey Coast Line route to Hazlet or get on the train at New York Penn Station. The seat next to me usually sat empty, even on a crowded train. Not until I read a 2010 *New York Times* op-ed by John Edgar Wideman headlined "The Seat Not Taken" did I understand that I was neither crazy nor alone in experiencing this.

The drain of the commute—the early to wake, work all day, maybe go out with friends after work, late to bed routine— manifested itself the first Friday home after my first week at work. Still in my coat, I sat on my bed to read a long-awaited letter from a college friend. I woke the next morning fully dressed, still in my coat with the letter still in my hand. It would be another six months before that would change.

It was early January 1991. I was sitting at my desk watching a snowstorm crawl over New Jersey, slowly making its way to the Hudson River, when a relatively new friend called me at the office. He knew I was looking for an apartment in the city and gave me the address of an available studio apartment: 81 Jane Street. If my high school years in Newark were dissonant because of the wide gap between what I wanted my life to be and what it was, then closing that gap would start by moving to the West Village. Jane is one of those streets where creativity swirls around you and history sits right under your nose. Alexander Hamilton died in a home that once sat atop what is now 82 Jane Street after his ill-fated duel with Aaron Burr across the river in New Jersey.

Snow started floating to earth over Manhattan as I walked to the Chambers Street station to make my way there. The true beauty of Jane Street didn't reveal itself until after I crossed Eighth Avenue and then Ninth Avenue. The hustle and bustle of people and cars and taxis receded, and I arrived at the tranquil corner of Jane and Greenwich Streets. The scene that unfolded before me was downright cinematic, so beautiful that I pinched myself over and over again. I needed reassurance that it was real. The apartment was on a tree-lined stretch of Jane between Greenwich and Washington Streets. The sky was that flat light gray color that accompanies cold and snow. The slowly falling flakes made it feel like I was walking inside a marvelous urban snow globe as they covered the sidewalks and cobblestones in a delicate white carpet, making the red-orange bricks of the town houses stand out more prominently.

Jonathan Ned Katz, a noted historian and author of books about gay history and human sexuality, answered the door with his partner, David Gibson, a graphic designer. They were a delightfully odd couple. Jonathan was older, a smidge shorter than me, serious, and direct. David was taller, younger with an easy smile. They gave me a tour of the apartment, which was really a refurbished gem of a bedroom in the front half of the ground floor of their town house. But it had its own entrance through a little gate and then down a couple of steps.

The original thick plank floors were restored, the walls were pale yellow, and the fireplace and mantel were painted white. There were two big windows that looked out on the pedestrian and vehicular traffic on Jane Street. The closet was huge, plenty of space for all my clothes, but there was no kitchen. They said they would allow me to have a small refrigerator and a microwave, which was fine because they would do nothing more than store and heat up the microwave dinners that would become the mainstay of my diet.

I left the meeting hopeful that Jonathan and David would rent me the apartment. It would set me on my way. A home of my own in New York City, in a beautiful neighborhood that finally matched the vision of what I desperately wanted my life to be. A fancy city life with an important-sounding job. An independent life with a gay identity and someone to love. That was the hope. A few days later, Jonathan and David offered me the apartment. And I accepted.

The rent was just $500 a month.

CHAPTER 9

NATIVE
NEW YORKER

I was born and grew up in New Jersey, but I was raised as an adult by New York City. How I move in the world was crafted there. How I view myself in it was nurtured there. I learned the various rhythms of the city and reveled in being part of the chaotic mix that made the Big Apple grand. Moving to New York City was the ultimate bet on myself.

New York City is like an M&M, hard on the outside, soft on the inside. That tough outer shell easily intimidates. The crowds. The congestion. The sky-high buildings with their sky-high prices. The big rent checks for small apartments. The startling disparities between rich and poor in a city teeming with ambition.

But that outer shell is easily broken by anyone who dares to try to make New York City their own. Those who do discover that the big bad city is really a series of small towns created by their own daily routines and Venn diagram–like social circles. Patterns and people emerge that end up making the city feel familiar, feel like home.

New York City demands that you bet on yourself. It teaches you that when someone asks you what you want, you tell them. It will build you up and celebrate your successes. And it will smack you down and magnify your failures and insecurities. Most of all, it is a city that rewards the resilient, the people who fight for their place in its glittering madness. The five boroughs are filled with them. Surviving that harsh cycle is what makes a New Yorker a New Yorker.

———

My small-town New York City took shape before I moved there in February 1991 and became defined once I had settled into Jane Street. My world didn't go north of 14th Street, unless I was going to the restaurant called 18th & 8th, a gay culinary oasis in Chelsea before it became the quintessential gayborhood in the mid-1990s, or to the apartment of the sexy Morrison and Foerster lawyer I was seeing. Nor did it go south of the Municipal Building, where I worked.

Tom Morgan wasn't kidding when he said my job at WNYC would entail long hours. As his assistant for public affairs, I wrote his speeches and many memos, but my main duty was to work with the board of directors, primarily as the keeper of the minutes. This was a who's who board of New York City insiders. A working board chaired by Wilma "Billie" Tisch, a petite woman with small round stylish reading glasses sometimes perched on her nose who ran an efficient meeting.

It was in this job that I learned you can never be overprepared. As Tom's liaison to the board, I went to every committee and subcommittee meeting. One day, we were at a committee meeting where Billie asked about something from another committee. The answer lay within a file back at the office. She was fine that I didn't have the answer right away. But I never allowed myself to be caught unprepared again. From then on, I carried a WNYC tote bag stuffed with every relevant file for every committee. It weighed a ton, but came in handy more times than I can remember.

I observed Billie intently in this job. I paid attention to how she interacted with people. I watched how she dealt with different situations. In all instances, she was gracious. I admired how focused she was on ensuring WNYC's future. Mostly, I marveled at how unassuming she was, given who she is. Billie's husband was Laurence "Larry" Tisch, the cofounder of the Loews Corporation and, at the time, the chairman and CEO of CBS.

One evening after a committee meeting at the Tisches' Fifth Avenue apartment, which looked out on the Metropolitan Museum of Art, Billie asked if I wanted a ride downtown, since she was headed to NYU. I accepted. The walk from Washington Square Park to Jane was not a long one. Billie said we just needed to pick up Mr. Tisch, who was waiting down the street. I imagined a chauffeur-driven limousine or some other luxury conveyance. "Right this way, Mrs. Tisch," said the doorman as he guided us to her Chevy Caprice wood-paneled station wagon.

My dreams of getting into television news never died. After nearly two really good years at WNYC, I made a move that would get me back on track. I took two weeks off from WNYC to work as a vacation relief staffer on the *Today* show. Many of the people I worked with during my internship days were still there. And I made new friends. Key among them was an out gay twenty-something African American wunderkind named James Blue.

If anything popped off anywhere around the world in the early 1990s, Jeff Zucker, then the executive producer of the *Today* show, sent James to be the researcher on the ground. That put James in places like Haiti and Somalia. It was during the LA riots in 1992 after the acquittal of the officers who beat Rodney King during a traffic stop the year before that James phoned me. Nothing major. A simple catch-up call in which he said he was tired and how he wished the senior producer would hire more people.

"Where do I send my résumé? I'm interested," I said. "Are you serious?" James replied. When I answered in the affirmative, he told me to send my résumé to Beth O'Connell, the *Today* show's senior producer. I did as instructed and landed an interview. On that late June 1992 afternoon, I was ushered into her office and was thrilled to see Mary Alice O'Rourke, my internship den mother sitting on the sofa. Throughout the interview, one producer after another walked in to give a status report on their segments, only to stop mid-sentence to thrill over seeing me and sing my praises to a woman I'd never met before.

Less than a week later, the day before my twenty-fifth birthday, Beth called with a question: "How would you like to come back to the *Today* show?" Those two summer internships at

Today during college, when I worked for free, was a bet on myself that paid off. This would be another. The job at *Today* matched what I was making at WNYC. But it was only a six-month vacation relief gig with no health insurance. I could get re-upped after the six months, but there was no guarantee. I ended up staying for nearly a year.

My desk at 30 Rock was in a sliver of an office space just down the hall from the bathroom where Gene Shalit taught me how to tie a bow tie. My office mate was a beautiful young woman from Missouri with blond hair and those Ferragamo flats with bows on the toes. Now that I was a researcher, no more casting about for assignments. They came our way in a torrent. Being in the news business meant your time was not your own. You worked late nights and endured truncated weekends to nail down stories and firm up segments. And breaking news could make you late for dinner or a movie, if not force you to cancel your plans altogether. All for the privilege of being a journalist.

As researchers, we also acted as bookers. Dialing up prospective guests to get them to come on the show before *Good Morning America* could. When Supreme Court Justice Thurgood Marshall died on January 24, 1993, I was tasked with calling former Tennessee Senator Al Gore Sr. His wife answered the phone. My telling her why I was calling was the first she'd heard that the man her husband voted to confirm as the first African American to the nation's highest court had passed away. During the fifty-one-day standoff between federal law enforcement and David Koresh, leader of the Branch Davidian cult, I was in regular contact with his grandmother Jean Holub. I raced out of a staff meeting on March 31, 1993, when news broke that the compound in Waco, Texas, was on fire. "We're all just crying," Jean told me over the phone. "This is so terrible." I never succeeded in getting her to come on the show.

And then there were the pitches we came up with that turned into television. My crowning achievement was getting RuPaul on the show. His song "Supermodel" became an instant gay anthem and was one of the tunes on a loop in my head as I sliced through the chilly water at the Carmine Street pool. More importantly to me, RuPaul's album was unapologetically gay and unapologetically Black. I saw him as a harbinger of things to come culturally and desperately wanted to get him in full regalia on the show. My wish to have RuPaul live on the show was rejected, but a remote shoot was green-lit with entertainment correspondent Jill Rappaport. We shot the interview at the Supper Club on 47th Street in the summer of 1993. RuPaul was everything I hoped he'd be. Charming. Fun. And visionary.

Of all the stories I worked on, the twenty-fifth anniversary of the assassination of the Reverend Dr. Martin Luther King Jr. was the most memorable. I flew with Bryant Gumbel and producer Jack Chestnut on March 31, 1993, to Riverhead Maximum Security Institution in Nashville for Bryant's interview with James Earl Ray. When the man convicted of the murder of the civil rights leader was escorted into the room, Bryant was gracious in his welcome and thanked him for agreeing to the sit-down. But when Ray extended his hand, Bryant said, "You will understand if I do not shake your hand." Ray said he understood.

Another duty of a researcher is to pre-interview prospective guests to not only gauge their veracity or knowledge, but also determine how well they might do on television. Then, I wrote up my pre-interview notes as stories, a full narrative about the pre-interview guest that incorporated all the information the lead researcher and producer would need.

My notes took longer than anyone else's and earned me more than a few stern messages demanding to know where they were. But often, I would get a message from the lead researcher or the producer, sometimes even from Bryant or Katie Couric, complimenting my notes. Anytime that happened, I put the lauded research note in a file folder. What possessed me to do that, I don't know. But it proved a smart move.

In January 1993, real estate magnate Mortimer Zukerman and business partner Fred Drasner bought the *Daily News* for $36 million. Six months or so later, my office phone rang. The man on the other end identified himself as Bob Laird, opinion editor for the *New York Daily News*. He said the new publisher was looking for young people who could write for the editorial page and told me that he got my name from his friend Tom Morgan, my old boss. When Tom was Mayor John Lindsay's press secretary, Bob was Tom's deputy.

"Tom told me you were having too much fun at NBC and probably wouldn't be interested," Bob said in his characteristically modest way. The whole notion of the call seemed insane to me. I'm finally in television, where I longed to be my entire life. And now here's this guy asking me if I wanted to go into the newspaper business. No thanks.

"He's right," I said, affirming Tom's assessment of my happiness with my current employment. There was something about Bob's tone in response—a mix of disappointment and "Are you sure?!"—that struck me. So much so, I called my mom and my boyfriend. While I phoned them separately, they had the same response: "Are you crazy? Call him back! See what he wants. You don't even know what the job is."

Bob and I met for lunch a few days later. He told me about the job and asked if I had any writing samples. That's when I told him about my file of research notes as news stories. He asked me to send him some of them, and the next thing I know, I'm sitting in a conference room in the legendary *Daily News* art deco headquarters on 42nd Street. The two men seated at the conference table were sleeves-rolled-up newspapermen. Arthur Browne, a handsome mix of Steve McQueen and Ed Harris, was the editorial page editor. His deputy was Michael Goodwin, a former City Hall bureau chief for the *New York Times*. Goodwin's boyish face was quick to smile, which made him the good cop to Browne's bad cop in our meeting. They were a reporting editorial board, meaning they didn't just pontificate from journalism's ivory tower. They did their own digging for news and information that informed the editorials they published. Their pitch was matter of fact. If I wanted to learn how to be a reporter and an opinion writer, they would teach me. "You're raw clay," they said, asking me to write a sample editorial on any topic.

They offered me the job. And making another bet on myself, I took it.

I made the jump to newspapers because of what *Today* executive producer Steve Friedman told me during my internship days. People from TV love people from print because they know how to think and they know how to write. The promise of learning to write was what was most attractive about the *Daily News* job. My plan was to do the newspaper thing for two years and then go back to *Today* in a higher position, like associate producer. I stayed longer, long enough to win a Pulitzer Prize.

Dating as a twenty-something in New York City then was a little scary for me. HIV/AIDS stalked the land. All I needed to do was walk through my neighborhood, into a bar or restaurant frequented by gay men, to be reminded of how tenuous my negative status was. Even if I met someone, I was generally too afraid to act. And when I did act, it felt like I was gambling with my life even when what transpired would be considered the most vanilla of sex.

Then there was Jeffrey Dahmer. What made reading the grisly exploits of the white Milwaukee serial killer who preyed on young Black and brown men and boys so terrifying was that he was totally my type. An attractive six-foot nerd with glasses and reddish-blond hair. I'm naturally reserved, not confident in my looks at all, and truth be told, painfully shy. If Dahmer had chatted me up as he did his victims, I would have basked in the attention. But his murderous acts sent my already cautious demeanor into overdrive. A demeanor that read as uptight, according to my friend and self-appointed mama bear Vernon, a gloriously grand Black and bald opera singer who moved back to New York from Paris. And it was turning guys off, he said.

That was hardly a new revelation. Trying to live an unblemished life—to keep my nose clean, as my mother warned—made me uncomfortable in situations commonplace for a twenty-something. Pot smoke sent me scrambling out of a room. I never put myself in a situation where any drug use more advanced than alcohol might be present. Thus, my efforts to live a life beyond reproach rendered me unapproachable. Still does.

But something else was getting in the way of me meeting someone special: I wasn't Black enough. Not Black enough for

Black men who thought me too white and didn't give me the time of day. Not Black enough for white men into "real" Black men who fit a thuggish stereotype I could never meet. How many times my irritation grew as I had to listen to someone marvel at how well I spoke. How many times my heart sank as I watched interest in me wane because of what I talked about. How insulted I felt when a white guy's first word to me was "Yo!" And then there were the white guys who so fetishized Black men that my value was solely dependent on the inches that lay beneath my waistband. I longed for a boyfriend. One who saw me as a quirky, complex, and whole person. On April 4, 1992, I met that person.

My habit of having a restaurant home started with Caffe Rafaella, a shabby chic Seventh Avenue café I frequented multiple times a week, where Julie, the opera-singing waitress, always hit a high C when singing "Happy Birthday" to celebrants. When I walked in that April day, Julie came over to my table and asked, "Have you seen the new waiter? He's Italian and he's HOT!" She wasn't lying.

When anyone tells me about romantic partners, I always ask, "Who would play them in the movie?" In the case of Giuseppe, the twenty-nine-year-old Italian architect from Naples with thick black hair and a big smile, it would be George Clooney from his days on *ER*. He was impossibly handsome. Certainly too handsome to be interested in an ugly duckling like me. But each time I came into the restaurant, Giuseppe paid attention to me, even when I wasn't in his section.

Julie assured me Giuseppe was interested. He was just waiting for me to make the first move. Not my forte, as exhibited by the words that came out of my mouth when I finally worked up the courage to make that move. "So, Giuseppe," I nervously asked, "what do you do when you're not here?" Of course, I already knew the answer. Julie made sure of that. He and another architect from Naples were opening a studio in the Meatpacking District. The building was just a few blocks north of my Jane Street apartment.

Giuseppe and I exchanged phone numbers. When we finally spoke a week later, on April 11, he proposed we have dinner that night. No good. I had a dinner party at Ricardo's in Hoboken. Nor were any of the other nights proposed by Giuseppe, who said, "Well, maybe some other time." I could hear the disappointment in his voice and feel the disappointment in myself for getting in my own way. But I had an idea. If he was going to be at his studio, I could swing by and say hi since it was close by. Giuseppe, his tone and enthusiasm perked up, said sure.

One of the funniest scenes in the 1972 movie *What's Up, Doc?* is when Eunice Burns, played by Madeline Kahn, is erroneously told by Judy Maxwell, played by Barbra Streisand, to go to 459 Dirella Street for a luncheon being hosted by Frederick Larrabee. After getting out of the taxi, Burns nervously asks the taxi driver if he was sure she was at the right address. He confirms that it is and peels off even after she requests that he wait. The scene widens out to reveal a ramshackle wooden two-story building on a loading dock in San Francisco Bay. With debris crunching under her feet after climbing the warped and untethered stairs to the second floor in her pristine Tiffany blue color-coordinated dress and shoes, Burns repeatedly calls out "Hello" in that quiet, unsure tone when one is truly scared to death. That was me climbing the uneven, shaky, and debris-filled stairs of 55 Little West 12th Street.

The 1100-square-foot loft was filled with light and smelled of paint and turpentine when I walked through the metal door at the top of the third floor. Thanks to a great deal from the landlord, Giuseppe and his architecture partner, Ada, a natural beauty who shared his passion for their profession and New York City, got a year of free rent and then a very low monthly rent in exchange for fixing up the place. Giuseppe's plan was to live there while they turned it into their architecture office.

Touring me around, Giuseppe showed me where the kitchen and shower would go along the back wall, where the windows looked out on other buildings, including the huge Mars dance club. Then he walked me to the front windows. The view looked out over Little West 12th and the loading dock of the Gansevoort Market Meat Center across the street. Those windows also had a view of the towers starting to line the New Jersey side of the Hudson River that afforded those residents a priceless view of Manhattan. And there, between the first and second windows, Giuseppe kissed me.

I called Ricardo to ask if Giuseppe could come to dinner. He readily said yes and that he or his boyfriend, Carlos, would pick us up at the Hoboken PATH station. Giuseppe and I waited for someone to arrive for forty-five minutes, an eternity when you're with someone you've just met, have been intimate with, and are praying you don't say or do anything to douse the flame. But our conversation during that wait ran the gamut, from his dream of challenging architecture and design with a firm he called LOT-EK to the verboten first-date topics of what and who we were looking for. All our cards were on the table by the time we were picked up. We were looking for each other.

Because Giuseppe was living with Ada and her Jamaican fiancé, Terence, in Brooklyn, he would come to 81 Jane after closing at Caffe Rafaella. I would leave the key on top of the outdoor light under the stairs. The squeak of the gate, the turn of the key, let me know he was back. This went on for weeks. He moved in a little more than a month after that first kiss, after I found a plastic bag containing a toothbrush, toothpaste, and a change of clothes hidden behind a piece of furniture.

I was totally smitten with this beautiful Italian man who said to me every day in Italian and English, "*Ma quanto sei bello*" and "You are so beautiful." He looked me in the eye when he said it. He said it so often and with such passion that I began to believe him. Believe that I was beautiful. I had never thought of myself in those terms. I never thought of myself as attractive, let alone beautiful. I was an ugly duckling hoping someone would see enough of something in me to want to make a go of it. What I got was a man who made me look in the mirror of his adoring words to see what he saw. Because of his love, I learned to love myself. The best, most enduring gift I have ever or will ever receive.

And it was Giuseppe, two months after our meeting, who told me to follow my dream and take the *Today* show researcher job.

When your birthday is in the summer, you're used to not having the blowout confectionary classroom celebration bestowed on your friends lucky enough to have been born during school months. When your birthday is two days before the Fourth of July, you're used to your big day being overshadowed if not outright forgotten. That didn't happen on July 2, 1992.

Giuseppe and I had been dating less than three months and were already living together. We were still lying on my rickety futon, which sat close to the windows, and the blinds were still down when I heard the ring of a bicycle bell and someone yell, "De-LEE-ver-EEE!" Lifting the blind closest to me, I peeked outside and saw Ada standing there, and I announced to Giuseppe, "Ada is here!"

Giuseppe said, "I wonder why?"

Donning my robe, I dashed outside and greeted her with a kiss on each cheek, the customary Italian greeting that was quickly becoming my own. Then I started babbling. Ada has these engaging eyes and ready smile nestled into a face that pulls you in the moment she says, "*Ciao! Come stai?*" And in the short time I'd known her, I'd grown to adore her. I didn't even notice what she was holding. "Here, this is for you," she said. My eyes finally focused on her hands holding a brand-new bike with a basket filled with flowers. I gasped and started crying. Giuseppe's thoughtfulness took my breath away, but it also meant the realization of a desire of his. Giuseppe had been talking about how beautiful it would be to bicycle around the city, to see it out in the open, all around you. That day we were riding around Manhattan amid the skyscrapers, flowing with the traffic.

I always smile when I think back on those early days. Days when we were rich in plans for the future and flat broke financially. Giuseppe was waiting tables during the day. My job with the fancy title came with a tiny salary. More than a few times, the only restaurant we could afford was the Manatus Diner on Bleecker Street. Didn't matter. We were together.

My first trip to Italy, which was my first trip to Europe, was for Ada's and Terence's wedding in October 1992. The civil ceremony was held at city hall in Maratea, a beautiful village about 130 miles south of Naples, where Ada's mother, a regal woman whose beauty was transferred to her daughter, and extended family have summer homes. I learned on that trip how loved Giuseppe was. Masina had us over for dinner at her apartment in Naples. A sprawling home on Via Posillipo with windows that gave her a front-row seat to the visual drama of Mount Vesuvius and the Gulf of Naples. Ada wasn't there, but old school friends of Ada's and Giuseppe's were. Masina doted on Giuseppe as if he were her own child. They told funny stories about him and cheered on Giuseppe's and Ada's pursuit of their own architecture studio in New York. Before we could even drive away, I dissolved into an ugly cry. Not because of anything bad. There was so much love in that room. The feeling of home was simply overwhelming.

Giuseppe had told me about the Posillipo home he left for America. None of what he told me did it justice.

Before me, after pushing open the courtyard door, was a green lawn with white pebble pavers leading to the house, a tall, three-storied white box with blue-tiled trim at the top, a terrace off the third floor, big windows on the first and second floors. Perfectly centered in the foreground was a tall palm tree, whose fronds splayed out like a permanently exploded firework. The interior was equally stunning, a postmodern twist on the Romanesque-Moorish style of a hotel in Ravello. As you climbed the steps to the roof terrace, Vesuvius could be seen perfectly framed within the porthole-style window at the top of the stairs. Once on the roof, you had a sweeping view of the Gulf of Naples and Capri, the ancient summer playground that sits offshore like a permanently anchored battleship.

It didn't take long for me to get the hang of Italian. I'd taken Spanish and French classes in high school and college, but Italian came more easily to me than French ever did. And I enjoyed speaking Italian more than I did Spanish. My problem was that I was too shy to speak it with fluency. Still, I could understand everything being spoken. Listening to Ada and Giuseppe every day helped. I also would buy *La Repubblica* from the newsstand and read the US news. Since I would already know what the story was about, it was easy for me to learn the corresponding Italian words and phrases. In the summer, we would go to Giuseppe's parents' house in Sant'Agata sui due Golfi, a town perched on the mountains between the Gulf of Naples and the Gulf of Salerno. From there, the Amalfi Coast beckons. The first time I saw Positano, all I could say was "Wow!" as I looked from the roadside at this medieval town dropping down to the sea.

On all those trips to Italy, I learned that Italians love a reason to celebrate. No reason is too small to gather people together. But when it's a holiday, a big deal must be made of it. So on that first Fourth of July together, Giuseppe and Ada threw a party on the roof of the loft, the nickname we gave their space in the Meatpacking District. On the weekends, Giuseppe and I would stay there, the odor of carcasses and dried blood outside clashing with the aroma of paint inside, evidence of their ongoing renovations.

The roof at 55 Little West 12th Street and the studio itself were the scene of epic parties and dinners over the years. There was the New Year's Eve party featuring a Brazilian percussion band that sent the packed house into a frenzy. Our friend Amy Bernstein arrived to tell us that there was a line down the stairs and out onto the street. Encountering the queue, she said, "Fuck this! I'm family!" and pushed her way upstairs. So many people came to that party that over the next few years, we would meet people who would tell us they were there that night.

There was the roof party we threw for Pride in 1999. With its proximity to Pier 54, we could see and hear the pier dance on the other side of the West Side Highway. When Whitney Houston made a surprise appearance onstage under the night sky, we watched the entire pier instantly go from roiling with the rhythm to undulating wildly, as if the chart-topping diva herself had cannon-balled her way into the pool of writhing bodies below.

And there were fabulous dinners around a big square table that could seat twelve, a dozen people invited because we found them to be sincerely nice and curious about the world and the people around them. Half would come from my world of media and politics; the other half came from Giuseppe's world of art and architecture. The music was usually jazz, either Disc 3 of *Frank Sinatra: The Reprise Collection*, Disc 3 of *Billie Holiday: The Legacy*, or the radio tuned to WBGO, the great jazz station in Newark. The dish was almost always the same. In the summer, penne with mozzarella, tomato, and basil. In the winter, usually orecchiette with broccoli rape and sausage. Both followed by a simple salad and a sorbet or ice cream. These were the kind of gatherings that helped us build a polyglot multiracial family of friends that formed the foundation of our social life in New York. A family that took shape at a party in an apartment in the East Village in 1992.

One of the guys I became friendly with at the Carmine Street public pool was a straight and handsome light-skinned Black guy around my age. Sometimes we'd go for a bite to eat or a drink after a swim. One day, he told me about a party some friends of his, college classmates, were throwing at another friend's apartment in the East Village. He was sure I would like them. With

Giuseppe back in Italy visiting his family, I was looking forward to it.

I had no expectations for the fete on East 6th Street, which looked like the edgy cousin of my relatively neat-and-tidy Jane Street. But what I found inside Apartment 5 was the home I'd been looking for. An apartment filled with young, mostly African American professionals who ran the range from nerdy like me to glamorous. They were talking, eating, and drinking. They were in finance, law, government, the arts, some of whom traveled the world for work or moved abroad and others who would repair to Martha's Vineyard, the Hamptons, Fire Island, or somewhere in Europe during the summer. They were as interesting as they were interested in the person with whom they were talking. The hosts were Maurice Russell and Dawn Davis. They could not have been more welcoming of the stranger who came at the invitation of a friend who did not show up. This apartment filled with Black people who shared my experience as a Black professional navigating predominately white spaces was an oasis where I could just be. Where I could relax my shoulders, let down my guard, and slip into that down-home patois deployed around family, around Us. It all felt like a warm hug, the kind I would get when I saw Grandma for the first time in months.

Lord knows I needed that hug. Since moving to the city, I had to contend with the soft bigotry of low expectations. No one expected anything of me, thanks to the negative images of Black men in the media and perpetuated by politicians. How many times had I watched surprise wash over someone's face as they learned where I went to college, where I worked, how well I spoke and dressed. Over time, my clothes became my suit of armor, used to deflect judgment and confound bigots. I would be lying if I said I didn't love shattering someone's preconceived notions or that I didn't love the "go'head" nods and smiles from other African Americans. And I would be lying if I said I wasn't exhausted by it all. That evening my emotions were akin to those of a lost kid in the mall finally finding his parents. Relief.

I couldn't wait to tell Giuseppe about the party, and everyone I had met there. I knew he would love them. During one of Giuseppe's calls from Naples, I declared, "These are our people! I can't wait for you to meet them." Not long after his return from Italy, I got us all together. A family was formed.

We were a tight crew. Black and white. LGBTQ+ and straight. American and Italian with Venezuelans, Argentinians, and French in the mix. The family growing with each new acquaintance or new love interest. We traveled in a pack to dinner and the movies. Gallery openings and museum shows. Beach houses and house parties. Some of my fondest memories originate in Maurice and Dawn's apartment, where dancing in the living room almost always broke out. Maurice played DJ and the songs he chose never failed to get people sharing memories and doing the dances that went with them. The bonds growing stronger one song at a time.

Whether in the city or on Fire Island, I reveled in the conversations that flowed around me, contributing if I could. They were so smart and funny. I felt lucky to be in their company, to call them friends. It was a wonderful, glamorous time. Personally and professionally, I was on top of the world.

CHAPTER 10

LEARNING HOW
TO WRITE . . .
AND WINNING
A PULITZER

Arthur and Michael at the *Daily News* were true to their word. They taught me how to write. On the editorial page, the print columns were double width, so lead editorials were 420 words. That meant the most important issue of the day, usually a complex topic that required deep explanation, had to be conveyed in the quickest and simplest way possible. It felt like landing a fighter jet on the short runway of an aircraft carrier. That meant sometimes our editorial board meetings resembled what I imagine the writing room of *Saturday Night Live* to be like.

Jokes bandied about until one hit on the right analogy that made everything click. When that happened, Goodwin would say, "Great, now we need to build an editorial around it."

My time on the editorial board taught me the difference between writing anonymously as the voice of an institution and writing under your own name as a columnist. Writing for the institution requires listening to everyone on the editorial board, melding all the points of view expressed around the table into a consensus document. The number-one duty of an editorial writer is to remember that you're not writing your opinion. And it took me a while to understand the power I had as an editorial writer. I viewed my job as writing what was right or true or fair. I didn't fully appreciate how the editorials I was writing were being received by the people working in the corridors of power. Their reactions could be quite something.

My first lesson in this came after an interview with the Reverend Jesse Jackson in October 1993. Like most African Americans, I regarded the man who was on the balcony of the Lorraine Motel with Martin Luther King Jr. that fateful day with a healthy dose of reverence. So as the taxi took the Triborough Bridge route to LaGuardia, I readied myself for my meeting with history.

Having flown the Delta Shuttle during my *Today* show researcher days, I knew there were conference rooms not too far from the gates, and I secured one upon my arrival. And then I waited. I scanned all the arriving passengers from the surrounding gates for Jackson's familiar face. What I learned that day was that arriving shuttles let travelers deplane from the back and walk the tarmac to baggage claim on the lower level. That's where I found Jackson. But he wasn't alone.

The Reverend Al Sharpton was there with him. His James Brown–inspired hair was as impressive in person as it was on television. Sharpton looked and acted like the bull in a china shop. His every utterance on behalf of African Americans, the poor, victims of police brutality and racism—"No Justice! No Peace!"—was meant to rattle the status quo. Wherever the flames of racism licked in the five boroughs, Sharpton seemed to be there to watch them, fan them, tamp them. I wasn't a fan. The interview was about a school initiative Jackson was proposing for New York City. One that a City Council staffer who'd lived in Chicago told me was a carbon copy of an unworkable plan he'd proposed there. Now was my chance to talk to him face-to-face.

But just as I was positioning my tape recorder in place, Jackson complimented my suit. I told him that it was the first designer suit I bought since graduating college. Then, Sharpton said something unintelligible that sounded like, "Whaaka na soooga waaaaa?" I asked him to repeat his query, in the hopes my ears would get accustomed to his rhythmic street-preacher cadence. "Whaaka na soooga waaaaa?" came the reply. What I heard was still unintelligible, but I took it to mean, "What kind of suit is that?"

I was so proud of that suit. A double-breasted navy blue with widely spaced pinstripes and peak lapels by Christian Dior, which I found on a rack at a Joseph A. Bank somewhere in New Jersey. Whenever I wore it, I felt like a million bucks. Whenever I wore it, people took notice.

"Oh! It's a Christian Dior," I told Sharpton in what I envisioned as the prelude to my going into all the details about what I liked about my purchase. Then, clearly and with precise diction, Sharpton said, "No. I asked you what college did you go to?" My face radiated with the heat of humiliation. My eyes were surely the size of saucers. My designer-clad body was frozen.

I broke the awkward silence when I replied, "Carleton College." Sharpton and Jackson burst out laughing. Each tried to outdo the other with a joke at my expense. "I went to the college of Pierre Cardin," said Jackson with a chuckle. "I went to the college of Yves Saint Laurent," Sharpton said, as the two prominent preachers dapped, pointed fingers, and slapped the table which I prayed to disappear. "Ha! Ha! Very funny. Let's get started," I said as I pressed record.

Sharpton didn't like the editorial that resulted from the interview and called Arthur Browne to say so. Calling me into his office, Browne put Sharpton on speaker as the reverend laced into me about the editorial. His constant refrain—"I told Capers! I told Capers!"—ricocheting off the walls. "Capers" became his name for me, which he said, to my mother's consternation, when we appeared together on CNBC's *Rivera Live* hosted by Geraldo Rivera the night of the Million Man March on October 16, 1995, my first live national television. Sharpton would tell me years later this was an intentional tactic to belittle me before the audience.

Ed board meetings, where elected and appointed officials; candidates for local, state, and national office; and other dignitaries tell us what's going on in their world, are illuminating events. Usually, these meetings are on the record. Whatever they say can be reported and quoted. But the visitor can also go off the record, their comments unreportable. When that happens, ears perk up and folks lean in. The unvarnished truth is bound to come out. For me, the most important aspect of an ed board meeting is being able to take the measure of the guest. Body language, tone of voice, tics, eye contact can communicate as much if not more than what they are saying.

In one particular *Daily News* ed board meeting, I truly learned the power of what we wrote. Judith Kaye was the chief judge of the New York State Court of Appeals, a formidable figure in New York legal circles. She was the first woman ever appointed to the state's highest court and the first woman to serve as its chief judge. She had a commanding presence and the dignified bearing befitting someone with her title, complete with a crown of carefully coiffed brown hair. Then I noticed something as Judge Kaye dressed us down for our editorials and the personal nature of the attacks on her. Her hands were shaking. A visual contradiction of the calm way she spoke.

In that moment, I understood the personal toll our writing had had on her. But I also learned how our editorials were making it more difficult for her to accomplish some of the very things we were demanding, things she agreed with. By facing down her fiercest critics, Chief Judge Kaye declared she was not afraid of us. And by doing so, she neutralized us and gained our respect.

One of the best parts of the *Daily News* space was the hall that stretched from the reception area to the main newsroom, lined with a gallery of historic, oversized front pages, from "Men Walk on the Moon" to "Nixon Resigns" to "Ford to City: Drop Dead." Touring dignitaries down this hall was a point of pride for the paper. But the gallery also included "Liar, Liar," "Impeached," and "Close, but No Cigar." All having to do with then-President Bill Clinton's sexual relationship with White House intern Monica Lewinsky. A discussion brewed over whether to skip that part of the tour when Hillary Clinton visited, or to remove potentially offending front pages. The conversation was short as

Michael Goodwin made the right call: If she's going to run for elective office, it is not our duty to protect her from what she will see in that hallway.

As Goodwin escorted candidate Clinton up the white-walled gallery, I took in the extraordinary scene. Clinton's face was like marble, etched into a permanent smile as she looked at the front pages, her head swiveling from side to side. And that smile didn't crack when her eyes landed on "Saint & Sinner," the January 27, 1999, front page about her husband's meeting with Pope John Paul II in Saint Louis. Witnessing that gave me insight into how tough a candidate Clinton was. Her subsequent meeting with us, where she spoke with authority on everything from mass transit to the dairy compact, proved that her much-derided listening tour was about learning the issues important to New Yorkers in all parts of the state.

Goodwin liked to get the board out of its ivory tower and into the city. A story in the *Daily News* on February 12, 1998, about how Governor George Pataki and Mayor Rudy Giuliani were battling with Representative Charlie Rangel over Empowerment Zone funding for the Apollo Theater provided the perfect excuse to go tour the famed 125th Street venue. We were greeted in the lobby by Grace Blake, the executive director of the Apollo, and two board members. As an avid viewer of *Showtime at the Apollo* after *Saturday Night Live*, I was under the impression that the theater was doing okay. It certainly looked great on television. But as they toured us around, looks proved deceiving.

Seats were broken. Paint was peeling from the ceiling. The carpet was threadbare in spots and dingy in others. The air-conditioning system was inadequate for a television taping, so the theater had to rent supplemental equipment. The sound system was out-of-date. That, too, had to be supplemented for tapings. The board was big on patronage and low on expertise in production and entertainment. Something wasn't right.

Goodwin asked me and Michael Aronson to investigate, to dig deeper into some of the details of that February story. We started working the phones, reporting for a solid month. Aronson focused on the legal side of the Apollo issue, chiefly the contract between the theater and Inner City Broadcasting, the company that produced *Showtime at the Apollo* for television. I focused on the politics of Harlem, namely its power players and how they wielded it. That meant I made it my business to go to everything happening uptown, every political event, speech, gathering. This was also a practical decision. Mistrust of "the white press" ran deep in Harlem, but trust could be earned by a Black reporter in its ranks. I worked hard to earn that trust. It wasn't easy. Being Black gave me entrée, but I had to dive fully into the intricate personal, familial, professional, and economic relationships that were at the root of the story.

My interest in Harlem politics had been piqued by a *New York Magazine* cover story a year earlier headlined "The Battle for the Soul of Harlem," about the power struggle between a cadre of young African Americans with business acumen pushing for economic development and the older generation as represented by the Gang of Four. Nothing could get done uptown without their help or input.

David Dinkins was the Manhattan borough president (1986–1989) who was elected the 106th mayor of New York City in 1989, the first African American to hold the post. Basil Paterson served in the New York State Senate (1966–1970), was a deputy mayor under Mayor Ed Koch (1978–1979), and then appointed secretary of state by Governor Hugh Carey (1979–1983). Percy Sutton served as an intelligence officer with the Tuskegee Airmen during World War II. He was a lawyer for Malcolm X and went on to serve two years in the New York State Assembly (1965–1966) before being elected Manhattan borough president in 1966. Sutton was one of the founders of Inner City Broadcasting, which had the *Showtime* contract with the Apollo. And Representative Charlie Rangel was the dean of the New York congressional delegation and in line to become chair of the powerful House Ways and Means Committee if the Democrats retook the majority after the 2000 elections. He was also chair of the Apollo Theater Foundation board.

As part of my reporting, I made myself a presence in Harlem and wherever Harlem players were the center of attention. That's what brought me back to 30 Rock, to the Rainbow Room high above the center of Midtown Manhattan, for an event featuring Deborah Wright. She was the executive director of the Upper Manhattan Empowerment Zone created from economic development legislation written by Representative Rangel and signed into law by President Clinton in 1994. She was also one of the people featured prominently in that *New York Magazine* story. But another person from that story would later become one of the most important people in my life.

I instantly recognized the serious face and round glasses of Darren Walker when the elevator doors opened onto the sixty-fifth floor. We didn't speak as I checked in. And as was my way, I took a seat near the back at a table that had a partially obstructed view of the podium. The spot wouldn't draw undue attention to myself, while also giving me a good view of the room.

Just before the event started, Darren plopped down in the seat next to me. The former corporate lawyer turned Harlem economic development do-gooder was funny, charming, and smart. Talking to Darren, I felt like I'd known him my entire life. Like I was talking to an old friend with whom I shared a history. Talking to Darren felt like home. Still does. That's the only way I can describe it.

With his help and that of Deborah Wright and others, I was able to understand what was going on in Harlem and at the Apollo. After a month of reporting, we were set to reveal what we learned in two full-column editorials that reflected Goodwin's wise counsel to eschew our customary biting commentary and simply let the facts do the talking. Not only was the theater a physical wreck and dark five or six nights out of the week, but the foundation also entered into a contract for taping the lucrative *Showtime at the Apollo* television program that was favorable to Sutton's Inner City Broadcasting. The board of the legendary theater that was the launching pad for just about every major African American star of the twentieth century was not stealing money. But its somnambulance was robbing the theater of its potential.

The editorials laying out that case ran on Sunday, April 26, and Monday, April 27. The reaction was swift. Sharpton called a community hearing, where Sutton sought to defend himself. At that hearing were the predictable cries against "the racist *Daily News*," and how this was part of a pattern of the white media going after three Black institutions: the Apollo, Rangel, and Sutton. I knew another part of my role was to visually blunt charges of racism against the paper.

Not long after his community meeting, Sharpton called me. "We need to meet," he said. "We" didn't mean the board and him. "We" meant just the two of us. This would be our first one-on-one since he crashed my sit-down with the Reverend Jesse Jackson five years earlier. When Sharpton arrived at the Stage Deli, he got right down to business, asking, "Why are you doing this?"

Sharpton and others had said that our campaign was meant to embarrass Rangel, Sutton, and the Black Harlem establishment. He added that the thinking was that the *Daily News* was going after Rangel as part of a hit on behalf of Governor Pataki to hobble his effort to be the next chair of the House Ways and Means Committee. All I could do was sigh at the absurdity of the accusation.

This had nothing to do with politics. I said, "Reverend Sharpton, you've been to the theater. You know it's a dump." I then delivered my sermon, which wondered how the crown jewel of 125th Street was sitting dark most of the week and falling apart. How the Apollo was saddled with a television contract that didn't benefit the theater. And how someone as powerful as Rangel hadn't found a way to revitalize the theater so that it could be part of the economic rebirth of the city.

Sharpton sat silent after I had finished my impassioned monologue. Then he said, "I believe you." He promised to stay silent on the matter and to be helpful if he could, a pledge he honored.

My Southern summers prepared me well for the two-year campaign to save the Apollo that followed. I learned how important
respect and deference were to elders. The "Yes, sir" and the "No,
ma'am." The "Miss this" and "Mister that." With the Apollo, the
importance was magnified because I was taking on a political
establishment weighted with history. I came to learn how that
custom of respect and deference could serve as a cloak against
accountability, allowing people to say or do nothing even when
things are wrong. Luckily for me, there were folks who were
eager to help me.

Chief among them was Evelyn Cunningham, the Apollo
board member who took us on that first tour. She was a strik-
ing figure. A tall, thin, and elegantly dressed eighty-two-year-old
in heels. She was also a Harlem legend. Evelyn ("You can call me
Evelyn, darlin'") had been a special assistant to Nelson Rockefeller when he was governor of New York and then when he was
vice president of the United States. But at her core, Evelyn was a
journalist. She was a chronicler of the civil rights movement as
a reporter for the *Pittsburgh Courier,* an influential Black newspaper she worked for starting in 1940. She covered a young
Martin Luther King Jr. and Malcolm X. She reported on the
NAACP court cases argued by Thurgood Marshall. She told me
how she once tried to interview Bull Connor and how he brushed
her off, calling her a nigger in the process.

In many ways, she joined me and Michael Aronson as a third
reporter on the story. As an African American, she understood
what it meant that I was the one helping to lead the charge to

change the Apollo. No one from the board would talk to me, but Evelyn would. Every day, sometimes multiple times a day, for two years. And she talked to the people who wouldn't talk to me.

There was another former reporter in on the story. Randy Daniels was a radio reporter at a CBS affiliate in Chicago before going to CBS News as a correspondent. By the time we met in 1998, he had transitioned from journalist to political appointee. The Empire State Development Corporation was the state agency that owned the Apollo, and Daniels was a senior vice president, one of the highest-ranking African Americans in Pataki's Republican administration. As a former reporter, he, too, understood the importance of our campaign to save the Apollo. As a Black man, he empathized with the attacks I was enduring as a result of taking on powerful Black elders.

As a member of the broader Pulitzer Prize committee that culls the hundreds of submissions down to the vaunted three for each category, Goodwin knew some of the keys for a good submission. That meant we pushed hard to report and write until almost the very last day of 1998. In an editorial on December 30, we reported that Eliot Spitzer, the newly elected Democratic state attorney general, vowed to continue the lawsuit against the Apollo Foundation's board started by his Republican predecessor.

Goodwin had submitted our series for the Pulitzer Prize and, working his sources during the culling meetings, found out they were one of the three finalists for Editorial Writing. The Pulitzer culling process happens weeks before the big two-day April meeting when the Pulitzer board selects the winners. Goodwin was assigned to cartoons. He got on the elevator with another judge. They introduced themselves. Goodwin told us that when he said he was the editorial page editor of the *New York Daily*

News, she clutched the folders she held and said, "I can't talk to you!" Goodwin took that as a sign.

The dates of the full Pulitzer Board meeting were on all our calendars, April 6 and April 7, 1999. We knew that at any moment during those days, we could get "the call." The secret call that lets you know you won. I was a wreck in the days leading up to that April gathering. I could hardly eat. During those two days, we were like a litter of feral cats, wild with anticipation.

But the phone didn't ring on April sixth or on April seventh. The next day, not long after Goodwin went to lunch, his office line lit up. It was "the call." His assistant took a message. We anxiously tossed a Nerf football to each other to try to release the nervous energy as we waited for Goodwin to return. Back from lunch and informed he had an important message, he retreated into his office and closed the door.

Brian Kates, Karen Hunter, Karen Zautyk, Alex Storozynski, Michael Aronson, and I all hovered over his assistant's phone. We saw Goodwin's line light up. And just as soon as it was lit, it went dark. We scurried back to our respective desks. The call seemed short, too short. Goodwin's door stayed closed too long. After what seemed like an eternity, Goodwin emerged from his office.

The first thing I noticed was how red Goodwin's face was. I'd only seen it like that when he was angry, like that time early in my days at the *Daily News* when the news side messed with one of our editorials and didn't bother to tell him. This wasn't a good sign. Goodwin wanted to wait until everyone was in the room before he said anything. The only problem was that Aronson had disappeared.

Hunter joked that he was probably somewhere reading someone's mail. She swore Aronson was a spy because he knew so many things the rest of us didn't. He was so smart and befitting someone so brilliant, he was more than a little quirky. And she crushed on him the way comedienne Leslie Jones crushed on MSNBC's nerdy polling genius Steve Kornacki during the 2020 presidential election. Someone went to hunt Aronson down.

Goodwin stood behind his desk, face still red. I took up residence on his sofa, lying flat on my back and excitedly saying "I can't take it! I can't take it!" Once Aronson finally came into the office, Goodwin said, "Close the door."

The mood got real somber when he put his hands in his pockets and turned his back to us. As much as we wanted to win, we knew it was a long shot. As excited as we were, our expectations were in check. My eyes were trained on Goodwin when he turned back to face us. In one swift motion, his hands flew out of his pockets, and with a smile beaming on his face, he said, "We got it!" I went from horizontal to vertical, like a rocket. The collective roar can only be described as primal, the kind that comes when an impossible dream has been realized. Goodwin swore us to secrecy but did allow us to tell significant others and parents. The official announcement would be Monday, April twelfth. He told me to tell Evelyn Cunningham and have her come to the paper for the big reveal.

The pictures in the paper the next day captured the mood. Raised plastic champagne coupes, big smiles from Goodwin and publisher Mort Zuckerman, and a handshake between me and Aronson after Goodwin credited us for "pulling the plow" on the editorials.

Six months after the Pulitzer Prize announcement, Time Warner took control of the theater, and legendary actor Ossie Davis was elected the chairman of the Apollo Theater

Foundation's reconstituted board, which led Attorney General Spitzer to announce the end of the state's suit against the foundation. That the theater continues to thrive a quarter century later is a source of pride for me. We were right to try to save the Apollo. But doing so came at a price.

Lots of Black people were angry with me. Called me everything from sell-out to Uncle Tom for going after Rangel and Sutton. Over the years, members of Sutton's family have told me off in no uncertain terms. I have taken their anger in stride. I understood it from their perspective and on a human level. At an event a few years ago, one Sutton relative sought me out to let me know the impact of what I'd done to him. She called him a great man, an assertion I never disputed, given the historic life he led long before we tussled over the Apollo. But I have never met a great man who was infallible.

Protecting someone Black at the expense of the vitality of a Black institution was a twisted expectation from folks who try to enforce racial solidarity with pithy put-downs like "All skinfolk ain't kinfolk." The same people rightly demanding to be treated like everyone else by society expect a racial exemption for people they deem authentically Black.

CHAPTER 11

WHEN SOMEONE ASKS WHAT YOU WANT, TELL THEM

The Pulitzer Prize is supposed to be the key to the golden door of journalism. Win one and your phone is supposed to ring off the hook with new opportunities and offers for better jobs. That's the popular myth. And maybe that was the case for other Pulitzer winners. That was not the case for us on the editorial board. Karen Hunter and I marveled at the silence. But in one of our many conversations on the subject, one where I wondered why there was such a discrepancy between what we thought would happen and what was happening in reality, Hunter brought me down to earth.

"Why would anyone call you? You just won the Pulitzer Prize. You always look like a million bucks. You never complain.

People think you're happy where you are," she said. "If you want to move to something bigger, you need to let people know!" And with that kick in the pants, I started putting the word out. I was eager to change my city and state focus for a national platform, but I was in no rush. I wanted to mull over the suggestions and ideas I gathered. One friend insisted that I look at Bloomberg News, a suggestion I didn't entertain because of its financial reporting focus. After one of our breakfasts at the Regency, I relented and said, "Sure," to his offer to put me in touch with Matt Winkler, the Bloomberg News chief. It never hurts to talk to anyone who wants to talk to you.

Everything that could go wrong did go wrong the morning of my meeting with Winkler. My proper interviewing attire—a solid navy blue Brooks Brothers—was at the cleaners. So was the gray one. The skies cried buckets of rain. When you lived in the Meatpacking District in those days, cabs were hard to find. The one that splashed through as I was coming out of the door refused to stop. I sloshed my way to the E train at 14th Street, my feet swimming in loafers filled with rainwater. The subway was packed. All those bodies radiating heat and the moisture in the air conspired to fog up my glasses. The five-block walk from the 53rd Street stop to Bloomberg's 499 Park Avenue office left me soaked.

Because my face hides nothing no matter how hard I try, I must have looked a sight to the poker-faced, bow-tied man standing in the distance. I noticed him as I frantically tried to dry whatever I could with my handkerchief, muttering obscenities to myself. As I questioned why I was going through all of this for a courtesy call that would go nowhere, his outstretched hand confirmed he was the man I was there to see.

"Hi, Jonathan," he said. "I'm Matt Winkler."

Winkler was the cofounder and editor-in-chief of Bloomberg News, plucked from the *Wall Street Journal* by Mike Bloomberg ten years earlier. He toured me around the newsroom, showed me the famed Bloomberg terminal, which sliced and diced data for monthly subscribers who paid thousands of dollars for access to it. We chatted in a little conference room steps away from his desk. He knew of my work at the *News*. I asked him a few questions about the place. And then Winkler asked, "So what do you think?"

"About what?" I responded.

"About working here," he said.

I was surprised. This was supposed to be an informational interview, a look-see. Instead, the man was offering me a job. "Oh, I don't think that's a good idea," I said. "This is finance and economics, and I don't write about that. It wouldn't be a good fit."

Winkler's poker face pinched. He sat back in his chair and folded his arms, then his voice took on a more aggressive tone as he said, "Well, what do you want to do?"

This moment provided one of the most valuable lessons in my career. When someone asks you what you want, tell them. You never know what might happen. In that moment, I had a job I loved. I wasn't going to leave to go just anywhere. But I knew what I wanted and what Winkler presented was not it. I had nothing to lose. So I told him.

"I want to write a column once a week and go on television and talk about it like I do right now," I said, sitting back in my chair and folding my arms as I looked him dead in the eyes. The silent staring contest ended when Winkler excitedly asked,

"Why can't you do that here?" His tour of the Bloomberg terminal began anew, this time showing me the opinion section they had just started to give their subscribers more content. They had already hired two hosts for Bloomberg radio. He thought I would be a great fit.

I freaked out. I had every intention of missing that morning's ed board meeting, but I looked at my watch and said I needed to get back downtown for it. I thanked Winkler for his time and agreed to think about it.

Over the next few days, we traded emails and phone calls. Each one made the prospect more attractive than the last. In one call responding to my question about what he wanted me to do, he said enthusiastically, "How does this sound? Jonathan Capehart, national affairs columnist, Bloomberg News." Sounded damn good, especially his approval to travel anywhere in the country to report out a column and to go to Washington one week a month to learn that city the way I knew New York. But Winkler would not answer my many emailed queries about salary. An insistent email from me on the subject elicited a phone call. He said he never discussed salary over email because it wasn't discreet. But then he named a salary that was about triple what I was making at the *News*, including an in-house equity system linked to terminal sales. I asked to think about it overnight.

"Boy, take that job," Hunter later yelled through the phone. "If you don't take that job, I'm gonna take that job."

I bet on myself. I told someone what I wanted when asked. I was offered what I wanted.

I took the job.

By the time I got to Bloomberg News, I was already expert at what Matt Winkler wanted from me, as articulated on my first day. "Write once a week. Write twice a week if you want to. All I want you to do is be provocative and piss people off," he commanded. It didn't take long. Whereas at the *Daily News*, I had earned the erroneous reputation of being a neoconservative, I quickly earned the reputation with the Bloomberg News audience of being a "Jesse Jackson liberal," as one critic wrote in a message to me.

Mike Bloomberg, the man who started his eponymous financial data company after being fired by Salomon Brothers in 1981, was a ubiquitous presence at his 499 Park Avenue headquarters. The multibillionaire was known to walk around in his shirtsleeves when he wasn't hunkered down at his out-in-the-open desk. The formally dressed man had a decidedly informal interpersonal style. Everyone called him Mike.

Once, the elevator door opened and on board the tiny lift were Mike; Kevin Sheekey, one of his closest aides; and two other people. The elevator was so small, I had no choice but to give Mike my back. From behind me, Mike deadpanned, "Capehart, you must not be writing." Someone on the elevator audibly gasped. "Why do you say that, Mike?" I asked. "Because I haven't gotten an email from somebody pissed off about what you've written." I burst out laughing. He let out a chuckle and said, "I get emails from people all the time. Keep it up!" But my days of writing were about to come to an end.

———

Joining the Bloomberg universe meant rolling in rarified air. Because of Mike's philanthropy, there were several black-tie dinners and events a week. I bought a second tuxedo to keep pace with the invitations that came in. If Mike was in attendance, Sheekey was sure to be there. You couldn't miss him. He talks fast and moves when he talks. His eyes dart from you to over your shoulder to the sky in a mixture of room surveillance and excitement about the conversation, which is often punctuated by a distinctive laugh ranging from wry to joyous. If we were talking, it was usually about politics and, more often than not, me answering his seemingly random questions about city politics. Our conversations picked up after the November 2000 election and multimillionaire Jon Corzine's election to the US Senate from New Jersey.

We were in Washington for events around the inauguration of President George W. Bush on January 20, 2001, when we found ourselves at the Old Ebbitt Grill, across the street from the US Treasury. Sheekey's questions kept coming. By now, I'd pressed him more than once about the rumors that Mike was thinking of running for mayor of New York City, but this time Sheekey asked me directly what I thought about Mike running for mayor.

Now it was my turn to fire off questions: Why does he want to run? Will he run as a Democrat? What's his answer to those who say he's a bored billionaire looking for something to do? How will he respond to the accusation that he's trying to buy the office? How much would he spend? Where does he stand on the issues? And I ran the traps on things he should know and worry about as he contemplated a run. When I pressed Sheekey for an answer, I wasn't expecting his reply. "That's what we were hoping you'd help us with," he said.

Sheekey confided that Mike was indeed going to run for mayor and that they would like me to be a policy adviser on the campaign. My seven years on the *Daily News* editorial board gave me insights into city and state politics and policy. So it made sense a billionaire, first-time candidate would look to someone with my experience. I never thought in a million years that someone would be me.

Having covered campaigns from a remove, I'd always wondered what it would be like to work on one. Given my career trajectory, going to a campaign was the furthest thing from my mind. Until Sheekey's offer. I told him I needed to talk with Mike before I made any decision. Sheekey suggested that I first read Mike's autobiography *Bloomberg by Bloomberg*. Once I did, then I could sit down with him. A few days later, back in New York, Sheekey sent me a copy.

By the time I started reading *Bloomberg by Bloomberg*, I had gotten to know the man a little bit. He had a Wall Street trading-floor sense of humor where teasing was a sign of endearment. He had a big heart that manifested itself publicly through his philanthropy and privately through myriad acts of unbelievable kindness. The book revealed a self-confident man with blunt assessments of human nature, the education system, the business world, and politicians. I saw a few areas where I thought the Manhattan billionaire would get chewed up by rivals and the press. But the book also revealed a hardworking man who didn't take his success for granted. A patriotic man who felt duty-bound to share his wealth with his employees, his community, and his country. The authenticity of his words and how he expressed them were so compelling that after reading the last page, I said aloud, "He's going to win!"

I knew full well the obstacles he faced. A party switch from Democrat to Republican that made him look like an opportunist and ideologically promiscuous. An entrenched Democratic establishment with a 5-to-1 voter registration advantage. Insane wealth that opened him up to accusations of being a bored rich guy trying to buy his way into City Hall. Yet, when I said aloud, "He's going to win," it was an involuntary exclamation that came from the gut. I felt it in my bones.

Sitting in a conference room talking about the mayoral run and my role in it with Mike, Kevin, and Patti Harris, the head of Bloomberg Philanthropy and Mike's right hand if Kevin was his left, was a heady moment. Mike asked me to be a policy adviser and use my knowledge of the city to help him navigate the issues that awaited him. He wanted me to work with policy experts coming on board and take the lead in drafting the policy papers that would define his candidacy. It all sounded very exciting. But as much as I loved politics, I was hesitant to leave journalism.

Mike was hoping for an answer right then and there. He was eager to get started and wanted to tell Winkler at their meeting the next morning about my move. I asked Mike if I could think about it overnight. I also told him that I wanted to talk to Winkler about it first since he was my boss. He agreed.

But when I got to my desk the next morning, there was a message in my computer in-box from Winkler: "Talked to Mike. Everything is fine. See me when you get in." I was shocked. I was pissed. Then I noticed the red message light was blinking on my desk phone. It was a voice mail from Mike, saying he knows he promised not to talk to Winkler, but he was so excited about my coming to the campaign that he couldn't resist. He apologized profusely, acknowledging that he broke his word, and said he hoped I would say yes. A classic "better to ask forgiveness than permission" move. But I appreciated his taking responsibility for going back on his word. Call me a pushover because it pushed me off the fence to say, "Yes."

Sheekey said that decision made me the first person hired on the Bloomberg for Mayor campaign. That decision also saw me immediately moved from the newsroom to the sales floor on the business side of the building. Because the campaign had not officially started, I was part of Mike's company staff, taking marching orders from Sheekey and Patti, who told me to take advantage of the lull before things really got going to take Mike around town to meet people.

Our very first stop was the Hetrick-Martin Institute just off Astor Place in NoHo. The nonprofit was founded in 1979 by Dr. Emery Hetrick and Dr. Damien Martin and provides services to LGBTQ+ teenagers and young adults, many of whom are homeless. In addition to providing a safe place to eat, sleep, even do laundry, HMI is also host to the Harvey Milk High School, which it runs under the auspices of the New York City Department of Education. But my goal was not just to show him HMI. It was to have him meet Verna Eggleston, then the organization's executive director.

I had gotten to know Verna through David Beitzel, Darren Walker's art gallerist husband who was an HMI board member. A former city official in the Koch and Dinkins administrations, Verna's advocacy on behalf of one of the city's most vulnerable populations was rooted in a moral clarity that never failed to bring people to their feet. Her real-talk and no-nonsense demeanor made it clear that she did not suffer fools. She didn't have time for them. She had work to do. If you're not there to help, then you best get out of the way. Who better to kick Mike's tires than her?

Verna was initially skeptical when I asked her to meet with Mike. His billions made him seem out-of-touch to her. Besides, Mark Green, the public advocate, was all but assumed to be the city's next mayor after November's election. But she wasn't so skeptical that she didn't take the meeting. As I hoped and believed, the two hit it off immediately. The no-nonsense Jewish businessman asked lots of questions and the no-nonsense Black lesbian didn't sugar-coat her answers. Each came away from the encounter wowed by the other.

Long before this, Mike had started learning Spanish. He had a tutor and also flashcards that he took with him everywhere so that he could study in the car or in between meetings. Patti asked me to make flashcards covering city policy and facts for Mike so he could learn about the city. They covered a host of issues and topics. "Acronyms & political jargon." "Demographics." "Transportation." "Housing." "Public Safety." "New York Schools." One side of the card had a list of questions. The other side held the answers. I couldn't produce them fast enough. And he ordered me to come by his desk multiple times a day to quiz him. "How many languages are spoken in New York City schools?" "What does HPD stand for?" "How many agencies have control over city roadways? How many are under mayoral control?" "What is the average daily population of the municipal jail system?" "What percentage of city expenses is the city debt as of July 2000? What is it in real dollars?"

Mike is a good kind of competitive. He knew what he didn't know and wanted to learn. I had to ask him a question until he got the answer right. If he got the answer wrong a second time, he would have the answer and then some on my third try. Mike wasn't like some kid studying for the test. He was like a grad student looking to ace the oral exam. After three terms as mayor, Mike has his PhD in NYC. But we had to win a first term and the deck was stacked against us when the campaign officially launched.

Announcement day was June 6, 2001. The first official campaign press conference was at a senior citizens center in Queens, but his first appearance as a candidate was at the Harlem Renaissance Day of Commitment Leadership Breakfast. Once held under a tent in a parking lot across the street from the historic Abyssinian Baptist Church, the annual gathering of New York power that morning was held in the grand Great Hall of the City College of New York. Its host was the Reverend Calvin O. Butts III, the church's influential senior pastor. His political prowess combined with the Wall Street financial and Upper East Side social connections marshaled by Darren Walker, then the chief operating officer of the Abyssinian Development Corporation, made the breakfast a must-attend flex of Big Apple Black power.

Months earlier, Erana Stennett had been hired away from her senior post at the Central Park Conservancy to join Mike's corporate communications team to focus on his corporate philanthropy. A Black woman with a personality that is as large as it is warm and a megawatt smile to match, Erana was my outside-the-campaign work wife. Together, we prevailed upon Mike and the campaign to attend the event to send a message to the African American community that he wanted their vote. A signal of inclusion for a constituency that had been treated with hostility by the man Bloomberg was hoping to replace.

Erana was waiting inside when the SUV I rode in with Mike and campaign strategist Bill Cunningham pulled up. In the distance, a human wall of press with notebooks in hand, video cameras on shoulders, boom mics held overhead, and zoom lenses aimed in our direction. Unbeknownst to me at the time, the campaign had its own photographer in the crowd. The picture captures the "Here we go!" excitement of that moment. Mike is smiling. Bill is smirk-smiling. And I'm giving the "Can you believe this?" side-eye with a smile. A smile that disappeared the moment we walked into that human wall. From that moment until we got to Erana in the Great Hall, we were jostled around as the press jockeyed for the perfect shot and shouted questions at the candidate. We were off to the races.

I was a policy adviser on the campaign, but not the only one. Kathleen Cudahy was my campaign wife. If I came at policy through a journalism lens, she came at it by way of politics. As the former legislative counsel to the city council speaker, Kathy was a perfect complement for the task before us, outlining Mike's vision for New York City. From meetings with policy experts and campaign staff would emerge specific beliefs and policy goals. Then I would work them into a three-part document that would be a statement of philosophy, a laundry list of positions within the area, and a series of promises and goals. The papers were written in accessible language to ensure that people understood who Mike was and what he stood for. But voters weren't the only audience. The press was just as important. So important that I had a mantra: "Would Joel understand it?" Joel was Joel Siegel, the senior political correspondent at the *Daily News* covering the mayoral campaign. He was smart and a straight shooter. As a former *Daily News*-er, I knew that if Joel couldn't understand Mike's policy positions, then Joel's readers wouldn't.

The process was as precise as it was labor intensive. The papers went through myriad drafts read by dozens of people. Most importantly, Mike read every draft and required that each one note which number draft it was and the date and time of the current revision he was reading, even if it was a simple word change or grammar fix. Then, there would be an event to release the policy paper.

Mike brought the Bloomberg way from the company headquarters at 58th Street to the campaign headquarters on 56th Street. No offices. Everyone sat in the open at a desk, including Mike. My desk was situated so that I could see the bank of televisions spread side by side on the wall in the narrow distance. I was tapping away at my computer when I happened to look up and said aloud, "Hey, look, the World Trade Center is on fire!"

September 11, 2001, was primary day, the day that New York City would begin the process of moving beyond eight operatic years of Mayor Giuliani by officially designating the Democratic and Republican candidates to replace him in the November 2001 general election. I looked up as I walked to my polling station to cast my ballot. The sky was cloudless and so blue, you'd swear the city was domed by a sapphire. Still, the most beautiful morning I had ever seen.

Polls opened at 6:00 a.m., so I was able to vote and still get to my desk at campaign headquarters by my usual 7:30 a.m. At 8:46 a.m., everything changed. American Airlines Flight 11 en route to Los Angeles from Boston slammed into the North Tower of the World Trade Center. At 9:03 a.m., United Flight 175 en route to Los Angeles from Boston slammed into the South Tower. Those of us in the campaign office were watching on television when that second plane hit. Patti, Sheekey, Cunningham, and others huddled around Mike's desk watching the coverage after his return from casting his vote and a campaign stop. The tone in the office was hushed.

The World Trade Center so dominated the region's skyline that the towers seemed indestructible. You could bomb them, as happened in 1993. But there they remained. Unbroken. Permanent. Until we watched them crumble under that perfect blue sky. Then, Shea Fink, Mike's campaign scheduler who used to work for Giuliani, asked a question out loud that scared the hell out of all of us. "Where's the mayor?"

Whenever anything of consequence happened in the city, especially one involving public safety, Giuliani was instantly on camera projecting leadership and strength. That's what he did after the planes hit the towers. Giuliani was on television walking amid a cloud of commissioners, aides, and press in lower Manhattan advising anyone below Canal Street to evacuate north. Then, he and his retinue decamped to a makeshift command center at 75 Barclay Street. Yet no one had seen him publicly since both towers fell, and no one on the campaign had heard anything from him privately.

Losing the chief executive would have been another shock to an already devastated city. But the political ramifications were enormous. If the mayor died before completing his term, the public advocate would become interim mayor until an election could be held to fill the vacancy until the end of the term. The public advocate was Mark Green, who was running for the Democratic nomination for mayor and the man everyone assumed would be the next mayor. Giuliani's reappearance was a relief on a host of levels.

It's easy to forget that on September tenth, Giuliani had been a reviled figure in New York City. A leader of a public that had grown weary of eight years of public fights, strong-arm tactics, and his callous indifference to valid concerns raised by his critics. By the evening of September eleventh, Giuliani was being lauded as "America's Mayor." The swing from loathing to adulation was aggravating. I was ready for his mayoralty to be over, ready for him to leave the Big Apple stage.

The public polling of the campaign put Mark Green way ahead of Mike. But internal polling showed Green's lead was steadily shrinking by the day. Standing on the observation deck of the Empire State Building the night before Election Day, a bunch of us were looking south over Manhattan, giddy over the election to come. If the internal polling was right, we were on the cusp of defying the odds and the naysayers. We were on the verge of making history.

The suite at the Hilton Times Square on Election Night was huge and filled with people nervously waiting for the polls to close at 9:00 p.m. Then the results started coming in, not over the television but over the phone. Peter Madonia was leaning up against a wall. A phone on one ear and a finger in the other so that he could hear. "Someone get these numbers down," he yelled.

Lacking paper, Kathleen Kudahy and Kathy Neuhaus, an aide on the campaign, supplied their business cards to capture the numbers as they were rattled off by Madonia. Each card had three figures: the percentage of the vote in, the total votes for Bloomberg, and the total votes for Green. With the numbers jotted down in ink, Madonia told me to brief former Mayor Ed Koch, his former boss, who was sitting in the main living room.

The circle of people to be briefed grew as Governor George Pataki, Mayor Giuliani, and former Senator Alphonse D'Amato arrived. And I added Sharpton to the mix. After each time I briefed Mayor Koch and Senator D'Amato, I would slink to another part of the suite to update Rev and get his expert take. In the early hours, when Green was leading, Sharpton and Koch assured me that it was early and that the Republican precincts had yet to report. And when those votes came in, the excitement grew as we all raced from Peter to various senior officials reporting the latest tally that had not yet been reported on television.

In the face of naked skepticism and disbelief from close friends and former colleagues, I believed in Mike, what he would bring to the city. That he would be a great mayor if only New Yorkers would give him a chance. And now, with more than 95 percent of the vote in, it was clear that they did just that. Eytan Davidson, the ace researcher who played guitar in a folk band and taught me how to tie a double Windsor knot during the 9/11-imposed suspension of the primary election and campaigning, ran up to Mike's suite with me to congratulate him. Sheekey answered the door, the concession call having already been accepted, and simply said, "You better get over to B.B. King's."

We were still working on Mike's housing policy paper when he went from candidate to mayor-elect. Now, all attention was on the transition. I was assigned to public safety. Because Mike made it clear that Ray Kelly, the police commissioner under Mayor Dinkins, would return to the job, the real work was finding commissioners for fire, corrections, and probation, among other appointments.

What I wanted for my future was a lingering question. Patti pulled me into a conference room and said, "Of course, you're coming with us to City Hall" and then she told me to think about what job I wanted. I was honored but had no clue what I wanted. Communications director was Cunningham's. Press secretary was Ed Skyler's. Nothing leapt out at me as the perfect job. Perhaps that's because I felt conflicted. As much as I found going into the administration exciting, I missed journalism. How could I not? I was sidelined during the worst terrorist attack on the United States in history and I wanted back in.

Winkler understandably rebuffed my desire to write something in the hours and days after 9/11. But when I called to meet about potentially returning to Bloomberg News, he readily agreed. When we met, he already had a plan. He wanted me to focus on global poverty. "Spin the globe, poke your finger, and wherever it lands, you figure out the poverty angle and how to fight it then write about it," Winkler said. Writing columns on global poverty seemed like another dream job that would turn the world into my beat. I accepted.

I told Mike, Patti, and Kevin my decision. I thanked them for the incredible honor of working on the campaign, and they congratulated me on the new job.

On New Year's Eve 2001, the *Good Morning America* studio on Times Square was the site of a Bloomberg celebration. A party to ring in 2002 and herald the incoming Bloomberg administration. Five minutes before midnight, the doors opened onto the sidewalk, which was cordoned off from the crowd mobbing Times Square. We craned our necks up to see the crystal orb as it slowly descended. Closing a chapter on a horrendous year for the city and the nation and opening a new one with a new mayor and new hope. At midnight, I turned to hug and kiss Giuseppe and saw tens of thousands of revelers cheering and clapping together, their blue and red tube balloons making Times Square look like a roiling sea of patriotic Good & Plenty.

Hours later, we were seated on closely placed folding chairs with blankets and hot cider watching Mike take the oath of office as the 108th mayor of New York City from the steps of City Hall. I had no illusions that he would be perfect or get it right all the time, but I did know that the man I was proud to work for was in the job for all the right reasons and the city would be better for it.

CHAPTER 12

"F****** S***!"

New York City had built me up and celebrated my successes in ways I never dreamed of as a big-head kid in New Jersey. There was so much excitement and certainty in those early years. But the next five years in the Big Apple would prove to be among the most challenging of my life and career. Years where I felt like I was being stalked by personal calamity and professional failure. Yet, through the pressure and heat, I learned so much about other people and myself. And I learned one really important lesson: Never take a job for money.

Except for that soggy first time I entered Bloomberg LP in June 2000, I always felt grand walking in off Park Avenue. When I pressed through the revolving door at 499 Park Avenue on January 2, 2002, I felt like a conquering hero.

That morning, I was returning to Bloomberg News after a ten-month leave of absence to work on Mike's campaign. A successful effort that saw Mayor Mike Bloomberg that same morning reporting for duty at City Hall, four miles directly south of the headquarters of the company he built. I was excited to return to journalism. I learned a lot from my detour into politics, but I was eager to get back to reporting, even if it meant doing a different kind of writing. My new job as correspondent for global poverty made the world my beat, but Winkler flipped the script after I accepted the job. I would not be writing as an opinionated columnist, but as a just-the-facts correspondent. I protested, telling him that I had no idea how to be an unopinionated journalist. "Oh, it's easy," Winkler assured me. "Take out the *could*s, *would*s, and *should*s and you're fine."

Thanks to UN Millennium Challenge goals, addressing global poverty was priority number one back then. The problems were and remain many. A twisted embarrassment of riches about which to write. All I needed to do was narrow my focus. After a few weeks of reporting, I presented four topics for approval: the problem of street children with a focus on Nairobi, Kenya; the problem of hunger with a focus on Mozambique; the problem of obesity with a focus on Brazil; and the problem of counting and calculating poverty with a focus on China. Only the obesity story was not approved.

As part of my effort to learn the players in this new beat, one of the first things I got was a press pass for the United Nations. Already a term member of the Council on Foreign Relations, I attended every relevant panel discussion to listen, learn, and meet. I attended the World Economic Forum gathering as a vaunted Global Leader for Tomorrow. A nice honor that gave me even less access to the conference than my Bloomberg TV colleague Dylan Ratigan, who was just covering the events.

I had great hopes for my global poverty beat because Arthur Browne, the man who had hired me at the *Daily News* eight years earlier, was now my editor at Bloomberg News. As a writer, the importance and comfort of having an editor who gets how your mind works can't be understated. But it didn't take long for the red flags to appear.

Winkler's assertion that all it would take for me to move from opinion writer to objective news side reporter was to remove the *could*s, *would*s, and *should*s was overly simplistic. As an opinion writer, you are free to say exactly what you think, in the language you want to say it. In the role of news side reporter, I felt like I was under arrest, deprived of my freedom. I began to more fully appreciate what a former *Daily News* editorial board colleague went through when he did the reverse commute, coming to editorial writing after years of reporting on the city's Department of Education. Watching his experience was like watching the character Brooks in the movie *The Shawshank Redemption* adjust to freedom and life on the outside after fifty years in prison. Whereas Brooks hanged himself, my colleague ended it all by going back to news side reporting. I saw firsthand how seriously news side reporters take their roles as objective chroniclers of the events they cover.

Within a month of starting the global poverty beat, I was looking for my own off-ramp. One that would let me stay on the beat but do so with the opinionated freedom of a columnist. I made my pitch in a memo. A column every two weeks that would fall into one or more of five broad categories that ranged from how people are living in poverty, the forces that are keeping people there, and the big institutions charged with alleviating it. The withering response came the same day.

At Bloomberg, the conference rooms are all glass. You can see who is meeting inside. Those inside can see who is milling about outside. The conversations in those fishbowls can't be heard. Unless the door is left open. Unless one of the participants is yelling at the top of his lungs.

I walked into a conference room with Winkler and Arthur filled with such hope and left it humiliated. Almost every attempt to answer a question or explain something in the memo was interrupted by Winkler yelling, "How dare you..."

It was the kind of meeting where your mouth is bone dry and your voice croaks as you try to speak during the onslaught. The kind of meeting where your heart races with panic because you're trying to figure out what the hell is happening. The kind of meeting that leaves you changed, in the eyes of others and yourself. The encounter left me shaken. As a child, I hated getting yelled at by adults. When it happened, I shut down. I said whatever I needed to say to make it stop. In that Park Avenue conference room decades later, muscle memory kicked in. My plea to be a columnist soundly rejected, I agreed to keep at it as a news side reporter. I just wanted the yelling to stop.

———————

Landing in Nairobi in May 2002 was my first time in Kenya, on the continent of Africa. The security reports on the capital city that I'd read before leaving put the fear of God into me. All sorts of warnings about rampant thievery and admonitions to keep your car windows closed to thwart feces-flinging beggars irate at your failure to give them something. I did not encounter any of that. What I did encounter on the week-long trip was still heart-breaking. And one day stands out.

Through my reporting, I made contact with Homeless Children International—Kenya, a US-based Christian charity that ran a school outside downtown Nairobi. They did a lot of work with street children. The reasons for their proliferation were many. A chief culprit were the school fees imposed on students. Those kids whose parents can't pay can't go to school. In a nation where most of the population was surviving on less than $1 a day, that meant streets were filled with children. The jails were also filled with children arrested because they were deemed in need of special protection.

My day started at the Nairobi Stock Exchange, and I dressed for the occasion. Navy blue blazer, pocket square, jeans, white shirt, and tie. I figured there would be time for Robert, the driver provided by the hotel, to bring me back so I could change for my appointment later in the morning with Megan White, the young American woman who was the charity's director of program development. Time was not on my side. Either my meetings at the stock exchange went long or the time to meet the charity was moved up, but there was no time to go back to the hotel.

Our first stop was the Lower Kabete Children's Remand Home. A children's jail. They were like children everywhere: screaming at play and happy to receive visitors. A child introduced to me held out his hand for a handshake. So cute. Afterward Megan sidled up next to me to whisper, "Don't touch your face." Some of the kids had just had measles. In keeping with Winkler's mantra "Show, don't tell," I summed up what I saw in the opening paragraph of my draft story.

Charles Karanja has been incarcerated since November 2001. Guards watch over him and 63 male and female detainees. They eat in a dining hall made of cinder blocks with bars on the broken windows. Charles sleeps under a wool blanket on a mattress made of foam in a dormitory that stinks of urine. He shares the facility with a 17-year-old accused of murder. Charles is five years old.

Robert then took us to Kibera, the biggest slum in Africa. A sprawling warren of poverty less than five miles from my hotel. Robert had pointed it out to me on our way to the children's jail. Whatever life existed there was covered by the low-slung corrugated metal roofs that stretched for as far as the eye could see. It was a desperate place.

My eyes were the size of saucers as we trudged through the muck to get to the charity's facility. Hard-packed red-dirt pathways snaked their way through neighborhoods of densely packed homes constructed with sticks, stones, and dirt. Homes that lacked plumbing. Trash was ubiquitous. As were swarms of flies that hovered in the air and crawled over food and other merchandise being sold by merchants. May, an old woman Megan said hello to, was seated inside her kiosk, selling piles of those small fish like the ones Giuseppe's mother fried up during the summer and were eaten like potato chips. Piles that teemed with flies repeatedly landing and taking off like helicopters from the roof of an embassy under siege.

A big pot was boiling when we arrived at the two houses connected by a courtyard of rocks and dirt that slept thirty-two girls. Like a good host, the headmistress presented me with a bowl of

simmering beans she had prepared for the girls' dinner. Like a
good guest, I accepted her offer.

The next stop was where the girls went to school. A giant tent
that sat atop red dirt on a hill that overlooked Kibera and also
served as the dormitory for the thirty-five boys who attended the
school. By the time we started walking there, I had acclimated to
my desperate surroundings. But I gasped when I saw the hill we
needed to climb to get up to the school. It was cloaked in trash,
a juicy pile of refuse of indeterminate depth. I ran with a speed
I hoped would allow my feet to skirt above the surface, the way
the Road Runner did in all those Saturday morning cartoons I
watched as a kid. Inside the tent, more scenes of deprivation.

My reporting never got published. Not my observations
of and conversations with street children in Nairobi. Not my
notes from my interview with Kenya's then–vice president,
George Saitoti, or my visit to the children's prison or Kibera.
There were multiple rewrites. Multiple questions from Arthur.
Some were excellent but would have required a return trip to
Kenya, which was never going to happen.

With each passing day, the truth of my situation at
Bloomberg News slowly came into view like a Polaroid photo.
Whatever benefit of the doubt I was giving to all concerned was
obliterated in a contentious meeting with one of Arthur's bosses.
The picture was now clear: I needed to leave. It was just a matter
of whether I left of my own accord or I was forced out. And the
latter option was barreling toward me.

I was told I was being reassigned to general news reporting. I
was also told I would have to undergo writer training. The choice
being presented to me was a stark one: Accept a new job on the
news side or leave. By the time of this conversation, I was already

engaged in another. With Michael Goodwin back at the *New York Daily News.*

Goodwin is the one who truly trained me as an opinion writer, and now that he was the executive editor of the paper, I sought his advice. I was honest about what was happening, what I could have done better. Most importantly, I told Goodwin that I needed to get back to doing what I knew how to do and loved: writing editorials. He said he would see what was possible.

Over the course of several weeks, I slowly removed my presence from the Bloomberg newsroom by taking things home. When the time came, I didn't want to be burdened by having to carry anything heavy. I didn't want to end up like a legendary New York newspaper editor who was unceremoniously fired. According to a newspaper story at the time, her sacking was so abrupt that all she had to put some of her belongings in was a giant bubble gum pink shopping bag from a discount clothing store, which burst onto the rainy New York street where she attempted to get a cab. When my time came, I walked out with just my Rolodexes in my tote bag and didn't look back. But that wasn't the only thing I walked out with. Minutes before I left my desk for the last time to head up to HR to make my departure official, I received a call from Goodwin. I would be returning to the *Daily News* as deputy editorial page editor.

My departure from Bloomberg News would be the first of many humbling events in my professional career. I loved the job. I loved the opportunities it opened for me. I loved the life it afforded me. I didn't love how things turned out. I felt like a failure. This was the first time I was forced from a job. But my personal failure was masked by what appeared to be a professional advancement, a new job back where my print journalism career began. A new job that required me to take a 50 percent pay cut. A new job with my old colleagues in what I would soon realize were less-than-ideal circumstances.

Gone was the camaraderie exemplified by Pulitzer Day just four years earlier. The editorial page editor was Richard Schwartz, once Giuliani's senior adviser and the architect of welfare reform in New York City. Personally, I liked him. He liked to crack jokes, usually followed by a har-har jab of the elbow to your side. But as the leader of the board, he was horrendous. He second-guessed himself, which meant departures after 8:00 p.m. or later were not uncommon. Friday nights, when three days of editorials had to be written, edited, and typeset before going home for the weekend, were the worst. In my view, he didn't act as a buffer between the board and the various views and whims of the publisher, which is vital for the functioning of an editorial board. He was a yeller and dressed people down in public, which cratered morale. I despaired at what had happened since I left the editorial page and tried hard to fix things, but it wasn't long before I joined in the misery of my colleagues. It would take another eight months before salvation arrived with the return of Arthur Browne as editorial page editor in October 2003. A true manager and journalist was coming back to the helm. Arthur possesses such a world-class poker face that he would win a staring contest with the King of Spades. Yet, not long after his return, even I could see the strain etched on it. The section was so broken.

The turmoil I faced at work matched the turmoil at home. Giuseppe and I were so young when we first got together.

Approaching our tenth anniversary, we marveled at how far we'd come. Individually, we were rising within our professions. Giuseppe's and Ada's love of repurposing objects and containers for residential and commercial use was helping to gain them notoriety and clients for their architecture firm. They were commissioned to do the windows at the brand-new Barneys New York store on Madison Avenue in 1993. Fashion photographer Steven Klein had them do a design for his apartment in the Meatpacking District, which never happened because he ended up moving. But they did do a video/photo art installation with Klein and Madonna called "X-Static Process" in 2003. For me, I went from winning the Pulitzer at the *Daily News* to being a columnist for Bloomberg News to helping the owner of the company get elected mayor of New York City. And it was while working on that campaign that fissures began forming in longtime friendships. I heard what some of my closest friends were saying about why I decided to work for Bloomberg. They thought it was all about the money. Their strongly held views of my motivation, despite my strenuously arguing otherwise, felt like a betrayal.

Meanwhile, Giuseppe and I were drifting apart. We wanted different things and sought them out in our own way. The pursuit of those different things became too much, and on a bench in Hudson River Park in the shadow of the USS *Intrepid*, I told Giuseppe I wanted to break up. It wasn't an easy conversation to have, but it was one we both knew was a long time in coming. What kept us together was what has made it possible for us to remain close more than two decades later. At the root of our relationship was tremendous love and respect. And as we went about separating our lives and creating new ones, we made a promise to each other not to say or do anything that would jeopardize that friendship.

I moved from our one-bedroom to an alcove studio down the hall, which still gave me a sweeping northern view of Manhattan and the Hudson River. Giuseppe eventually bought an apartment that he renovated himself in Chelsea. The most painful sorting was of friends. Much of that tight-knit polyglot multiracial family we had assembled over a decade carried on without me.

So I strengthened the bonds of friendship that were developing with Joe Versace and Ashley Schiff. Joe and I had our vault dinners. I accompanied Ashley to an untold number of events around Manhattan, from big galas to smaller gatherings. Ashley enlisted help from me and Joe with her annual gala for Jazz at Lincoln Center at the Apollo Theater. The three of us, plus a few others, were a grand crew. Flitting about the city from one event or dinner party or restaurant to the next. We had a ball. And yet, I was miserable.

Despite Arthur's return, things on the ed board were still rocky. Arthur was parsimonious with feedback. I never knew if I was meeting expectations or doing the job the way he wanted. More importantly, the 50 percent pay cut that came with the *Daily News* job started to pinch. The reserve of cash I had amassed during my flush Bloomberg years diminished one dinner, one expensive Barneys, Bergdorf's, or Dunhill purchase at a time. I had to face the fact that I needed a higher-paying job and that doing so would mean leaving journalism a second time, for good.

Conversations with friends led me to a meeting with Paul Taaffe, the chairman and CEO of public relations firm Hill & Knowlton. The tall, charming Australian knew of my work and was keen on bringing my journalism expertise to H&K. He said that my inside knowledge of news organizations and my political relationships would be of great benefit to the company and its clients. The salary would put me back where I was during my tenure with Bloomberg News and the campaign. On the advice of a friend, I went back to Paul to ask for a higher salary given all that I was bringing to the table. He heard me out before shooting me down, saying that paying me the salary I was asking for would put a burden on me to bring in business right away. Something he knew I wouldn't be able to do as a newcomer to the field. But Paul praised me for having the courage to fight for myself.

I should have paid attention to the little voice in the back of my head. I didn't recognize it for what it was at first, but I started noticing when the internal murmurs would start. It usually happened when someone in the public relations business asked me a curious question: Are you ready for agency life? In the abstract, I was. So on December 6, 2004, I handed Arthur my resignation letter. I enjoyed working with him and was forever grateful that he took a chance on me back in 1993. But now it was time for me to grow up, I thought. Time to make some money. Time to be a businessman.

On my first day at Hill & Knowlton, that little voice burst into my consciousness with a blunt statement: "You've made a terrible mistake." But I discounted it as first-day jitters. Everything will be fine, I thought to myself. Paul Taaffe worked it out so that my first year would be akin to an internship where I would learn the public relations business. The expectation was that in the second year, I would begin bringing in business. "Monetize your contacts" was the phrase Paul used.

The very first sign of "agency life" appeared in the form of the time sheet. An electronic grid of hell sliced into quarter-hour increments. H&K was a billable-hours shop, which meant that every 15 minutes had to be accounted for, coded to a specific client account. Having an account number would turn the time increment green. Not having one would turn it red. My time sheets were a sea of red with the occasional green 15-minute dot. "Agency life" required a client code to do just about anything, from making a long-distance telephone call to using the Xerox machine. I didn't make a photocopy for two years because of those damned codes. I left all that to my assistant. "Agency life" also meant being at the beck and call of your clients, their unreasonable demands and outsized expectations, anytime, any day. That didn't bother me so much since the news business put me one calamity away from rearranging or canceling plans. What did bother me was the client's aversion to the truth. I once was asked not to come back to a media training for a client after a lunch break because I asked a CEO questions his staff didn't want him asked. So much for bringing the mindset of a journalist to the job.

Every morning, I awoke with dread. "Fuckin' shit" were the same two coarse words I spit out each time my eyes opened on the new day. Except for media trainings and the small retainer clients I enjoyed working with, I had no love for the job. My heart wasn't in it. I didn't like the push to "monetize my contacts" or to get clients to sign up for services they didn't really need. And over time, I learned a big lesson I've shared with young people ever since. Do not take a job for money. Doing so when you're in financial straits as I was can cloud your judgment, stifle that little voice in the back of your head sounding an alarm, and blind you to a marching band of red flags that the job isn't really for you. Some red flags don't unfurl until after you're in the job. By then, you realize that you're stuck in a job you can't afford to leave.

I started entertaining other employment options almost immediately. In April 2005, three months after I started at H&K, Peter Madonia, then the mayor's chief of staff, called me. They were looking for a commissioner for consumer affairs and wondered if I would be interested in interviewing. I came up with the vision statement Peter said I should have once the process got started. This was no formality. The position wasn't mine for the taking. Peter told me more than a dozen other potential candidates were being talked to. Nine months after the initial call from Madonia, I received one from Mayor Bloomberg. "Let me buy you a drink," he said.

When I walked into the Mark Hotel for our meeting later that day, I'd long known the job wouldn't be mine. In doing my own due diligence, I learned that the acting commissioner was doing a great job and was highly regarded. And if there was one thing I learned working for Mike on his first mayoral campaign and during the transition, it was how much he prized experience and proven ability over his personal feelings for you, no matter how much he liked you. Nevertheless, I went to the Mark Hotel. It never hurts to talk to anyone who wants to talk to you.

"Tell me, again, why I should pick you for Consumer Affairs?" Mike asked. I enthusiastically made my case, touting what I would bring to the job. But when he admitted his dilemma was coming up with a rationale for why the acting commissioner should not get the job when he was doing so well, I bowed to the obvious. I told him there was no way I would or could say that he should remove the acting commissioner. All I could say was that I would do a good job given the opportunity and that, no matter what, I was honored to have been considered. Two months later, it became official. I didn't get the job.

I was so eager to get out of H&K that I entertained any and all prospects and talked about them with my best friend, Joe Versace. Three days after I got the no-go call on Consumer Affairs, we had lunch. What I thought was going to be our typical breezy and casual laugh-fest turned into a bracing come-to-Jesus meeting with Joe in the role of Jesus. He told me that if I left H&K after just a year, people would think I was unstable as it would have been my sixth job in as many years. He said I needed purpose. He said I needed to hunker down and become known for something at H&K. He said, "You need to do more than just go to parties." Joe's face was stern. His tone was unlike anything I'd heard from him. His gut-punch of words were painful to hear and sent me reeling. But even in the moment, I knew he was right.

Since leaving the Bloomberg News global poverty job, I felt professionally adrift. Casting about not only for money, but also for purpose. More than a few people had told me to strike out on my own, to open a strategic communications shop. They swore I would be successful at it, but I couldn't see what they saw. I lacked the imagination to see what was possible. The irony of this is not lost on me. Growing up, despite coming from a family with no one in journalism, no one in television news, no writers, I could see myself as a television reporter, a journalist, and I charted a path for myself like an explorer whacking their way through a jungle thicket. But explorers lack fear. After nearly two decades of adulting, I had it in abundance. I couldn't see how to bet on myself.

Since Giuseppe and I broke up after eleven years together, I felt personally adrift. Bouncing from one dalliance to another, hoping it would lead to something more. A combination of my clingy nature and choice of companion made sure that didn't happen. My dating travails served as entertainment for others. Some of the stories were hilarious, like the fella who feigned a mysterious illness not to see me again or the white guy I met on Match.com who called me in the middle of the night after what I thought had been a successful date to inform me that he had decided to date someone else, a Black guy named Tyrone. After a while, the teasing and laughter started to feel like salt in my wounded heart.

New York City was smacking me down. It was magnifying my failures and intensifying my insecurities, which only made the circumstances feel worse. Friendships that were important to me were fraying or falling apart completely. Those closest to me were advancing while I stayed stuck in personal and professional uncertainty. It was like I became that messy friend who you can only take in small doses and under certain circumstances. So I withdrew. As an only child, I am expert in dining alone, going to the movies alone, being alone.

Peering out the windows of my alcove studio high above Hell's Kitchen, I wondered how I had veered so far away from what my career promised to be. How I had failed to see the red flags. How I had ignored that little voice in the back of my head. In all that pondering, I came to learn from my failures. Each one a searing experience that forced me to face fear, stare it in the face. Experiences that taught me a lot about people, what they are capable of, and how to act accordingly. And I learned a lot about myself, what my limits were for other people's treatment of me, what I was willing to accept or not accept going forward. Most importantly, I learned what I was capable of. As a result, I did as much plotting as I did wallowing.

I regained my focus on my North Star, a career in journalism, and I got back in touch with that energy that drove me as a child to get into that business in the first place. I jumped at chances that would put me back on track. That's what led me to get in touch with Cat McKenzie at WABC television about reviving *Sunday Forecast*, a segment I did on her weekend show during my second tour at the *Daily News* that looked at the political news of the previous and coming weeks. She agreed, and I gladly got up early on Sunday mornings for no pay to do it. I also guest-hosted shows on WNYC radio. A decade earlier I was working there as assistant to the president. Now I was sitting in for the radio station's stars, Brian Lehrer and Leonard Lopate.

I didn't know if any of it would pay off. If any of it would get me back on track, back in news. But years later I would see how the contours of another life lesson were starting to take shape. Everything we do is an audition for something else in life; we just don't know what for yet. I had no idea what role I was preparing myself for or when it would make itself known. I just knew I was preparing for something, and it gave me the hope I needed to press ahead.

CHAPTER 13

A SWIRL OF
TERRIFIED
EXCITEMENT

New Yorkers believe every word of "New York, New York," the song Frank Sinatra made famous. They live in a city filled with people striving to be "top of the list, king of the hill, A-number-1." And those like me who leave the Big Apple for elsewhere believe in our bones that "if I can make it there, I'll make it anywhere." How could we not when we lived in America's biggest, most glamorous, chaotic, and difficult city?

Everything I knew about Washington DC from my regular visits led me to believe that moving to the nation's capital would be easy. And then I moved there. It has come a long way since I arrived in 2007, when it was a sleepy town whose downtown streets were empty before 8:00 p.m. Today, it is a city teeming with fabulous restaurants packed with fashionable patrons who live in any number of the neighborhoods gentrified over nearly two decades. It's a remarkable transformation. In many ways, it's not the same city I moved to, except in one regard: the people. Washington is a tough town because of them.

For many of the people who land in Washington, it is the biggest city they have lived in. The biggest stage they have been on. Perhaps even the first time they have been at the center of the action instead of longing to be so from afar. Which can make Washington feel like a giant high school where the nerds rule the cliques. The close attention paid to the power players from the White House and the Capitol means too many are looking over your shoulder for someone more important to talk to or talking your ear off about how important they are or their work is.

One of the golden rules of the Big Apple is that your first question to someone you're just meeting should never be "What do you do?" It's akin to asking them how much money they make. Rude. Instead, "Do you live in the city?" or "Have you seen [fill-in-the-blank movie or exhibition]?" A more indirect way of trying to suss out where your new friend might fit into the multiple worlds you occupy in New York City.

In Washington, the custom is to lead with what you do. Name and affiliation. A custom I have studiously avoided, unless I'm introducing myself to an elected official as a matter of disclosure. I absolutely don't do part two of the custom, and ask "So what do you do?" Whether the conversation will continue depends on what you say in response. I have watched people walk away from teachers and social workers. I have seen their faces light up meeting someone who has a job that might put them ever closer to the center of power. And even then, a government title is no guarantee you'll be shielded from stunning rudeness.

My relationship with Washington and many of the people in it can only be described as complicated. In many ways, I love this town. After all, my career was saved here. I met my husband here. I have made some good friends here. Yet I've never really felt that I fit in or belonged here. In my nearly two decades in this town, I've learned some valuable lessons I'm not sure I would have learned had I stayed in New York, the biggest being the one that pushed me to leave the Big Apple in the first place: Go where your talents are wanted.

The instant message from my assistant at H&K was like that ray of sunshine that breaks through the clouds after a really bad storm. "Call Fred Hiatt," it read.

Fred and I first met in 1999. He was the incoming editorial page editor of the *Washington Post* and had an editorial writing position open. He had heard about me from some of the paper's brass who had attended the gay journalists convention the previous year. Over breakfast in Washington at the Madison Hotel, we got to know each other. Fred was one of those kindhearted, brilliant men who knew everything about everything, from a zoning ordinance in Montgomery County, Maryland, to the intricacies of the latest iteration of US strategy in any country in the Middle East. Hiatt was also someone my colleagues and I at the *Daily News* had beaten for the Pulitzer Prize for Editorial Writing in 1999. A subject he alluded to with a half-joking aside.

The position he was hiring for then, writing editorials about the goings-on in Maryland and Virginia, would require me to move to Washington. I couldn't imagine leaving New York—where I was building a life with Giuseppe—at the time, and Fred must have sensed it. At one point, he said, "I wouldn't want to break up a marriage." With one remark that I had never encountered in my professional life, Fred signaled an acceptance of my relationship in language that was metaphorical, since same-sex marriage was not yet legal.

That's as far as our conversation went. Eight years later, less than a week into 2007, he wanted to talk. I called him back right away. It could only have meant one thing: a job.

Another position had opened up on the editorial board. This time, it was to replace the editorial writer who focused on a host of policy issues, including the environment and New Orleans rebuilding after the devastation wrought by Hurricane Katrina in 2005. Fred said he'd interviewed several people, but he went to his Rolodex and came across my card. He told me that he remembered my last note to him. A note written a few years earlier, during the tumult of my second tour at the *Daily News*, an SOS for a lifeline out of that chaos. Nothing came of it.

Remembering that note, Fred said he went to the internet to find my old columns at the *Daily News*. He told me he enjoyed them and admitted to not knowing I'd left the paper and "gone to the dark side" of public relations. Yet that didn't stop him from calling. "I figured I'd take a shot in the dark and see if you might be interested in this," Fred said. Our conversation was terrific. He quizzed me on my interest in issues of climate change, which I pretended to care about more than I actually did, and my thoughts on post–Katrina New Orleans, on which I had clear opinions with outrage to match. At the end of the call, Fred said, "Well, sleep on it and let's talk tomorrow." On that tomorrow call, he invited me to Washington to meet the board the following week.

That day was magical. Time flew by. One minute, I'm listening to the familiar presentation of an editorial argument, the thrust and parry that comes with opposing points of view, the clear articulation of the paper's position by the editorial page editor. The next minute, I'm meeting individually with members of the board. The conversations ranged from getting-to-know-you to my thoughts on particular issues. My sit-down with Bo Jones, the publisher, had a "kick the tires" feel to it.

Whenever I travel, I submerge myself in music. Something to match my mood. On this trip, I rolled back to New York City in silence. I watched a rush of trees, scenic river views, warehouses, and waiting passengers at the next stops as my mind raced with one sure thought: I was getting the job.

Darren Walker and I had dinner in the days after Fred made the official offer. I was elated, but considering my money woes, I was anxious. My new prestigious post came with a substantial pay cut from what I was making at H&K. But Darren set me straight, reminding me that the cost of living would be lower in Washington than in New York. More importantly, the move would take me where my talents were wanted. My first day at the *Washington Post* was February 15, 2007.

The first few years were a swirl of excitement. I was back in journalism at a place whose gothic logo outside its L Street entrance provided the backdrop for a picture Giuseppe took of me fifteen years earlier. One of those aspirational "I'll work here one day" photos. Early on, I wrote editorials on climate change and the proposed legislation to address it. I also wrote about New Orleans, advocating for the Crescent City to be rebuilt better and with the federal government's support. This was more fun, more in line with my interests. Then I started writing about national politics.

It was thrilling to be back in the discussions that shaped editorial positions. I soaked up the intelligence and expertise that flowed around the table from the other writers and frequent visitors. And once again, I witnessed the power of an editorial board meeting to change my mind about someone. That someone being President George W. Bush.

A year into my tenure, Fred announced that the editorial board was being given an on-the-record meeting with President Bush at the White House. Not just anywhere in the executive mansion. In the private residence on the second floor. Because we would have only forty-five minutes, we narrowed the topics of discussion. The Iraq War and the so-called global war on terror would definitely be discussed since they were still being waged by the Bush administration. But there would be no questions on climate, my subject area. Our positions were aligned with the president's so no need to waste precious time on an amen session.

My jaundiced view of Bush was shaped by my years in New York City. The Democratic Big Apple was never going to like a Republican president, but the attacks of September 11 and his treatment of the city in its aftermath made it impossible to love him. I also came to Washington believing he wasn't the brightest bulb in the Oval Office, just a good ole boy who lucked his way into the White House. That our reportedly intellectually incurious president had taken a back seat to Vice President Dick Cheney.

All that changed at our meeting on March 6, 2008.

The president, gracious and taller than I had expected, greeted each of us as we got off the small elevator from the State Floor to the private residence. We were then escorted to the ornate Yellow Oval Room, where Fred sat in a chair to the right of Bush. The rest of us were arrayed on two sofas on either side. Members of the president's senior staff sat in chairs facing him and Fred on the opposite side of the room.

There was a little drama at the start of the meeting when Bush said, "So this is off the record." Fred pushed back, reminding all that the agreement was that this would be on the record. To which the president asked, with a chuckle, "Don't you want Bush unplugged?" Things got underway when he agreed to Fred's insistence that questions about Iraq and Afghanistan be on the record.

The clock was ticking down on our scheduled time with the president when he asked, "Who writes about climate change?" Stunned, I said, "I do, Mr. President."

"Well, aren't you going to ask me a question?" he asked.

All reporters have a question or two in their back pocket in case this very thing happens and I had told no one what I might ask. No sooner had I started my query than Bush interrupted me, saying, "I know what you're going to ask me." I was taken aback by his presumption, but to my surprise, he finished the exact question I was winding up to ask. Once he had finished answering, I started asking a follow-up question. But again, he cut me off. "I know what you're going to ask me now," he said confidently. He then proceeded to ask and answer my follow-up question.

That forty-five-minute gathering ended up being an hour and a half. One of the most instructive ninety minutes of my career.

Before and after the meeting, I didn't agree with a lot of Bush's policies, particularly his foreign policy. Still, I left the White House with more respect for him than when I arrived. Listening to Bush, watching him, taking measure of the man, I never doubted that he believed that what he was doing was in the best interests of the country. He was much smarter and more wily a politician than his public persona. As we left the White House, I couldn't help but think how much Bush reminded me of the Reverend Al Sharpton. Both men had damaged reputations and were viewed as clowns, to put it charitably. But both men were well aware of their reputations and used the low expectations of their political adversaries to get the better of them. Hard to get the better of a clown that doesn't exist.

But that swirl of excitement in my early years at the *Post* was a terrified excitement. Returning to journalism after a two-year hiatus left me rusty. I wanted to do a good job, but I was terrified of failing (again). So I read the papers, did my reporting, conducted interviews on and off the record and on background. I tried to come to the table prepared. And yet I was always panicked when it was my turn to speak, to share my latest reporting on an editorial or to pitch a new one. These were some of the smartest people I'd ever worked with, and their questioning could range from inquisitive to hostile, depending on whether I bumped into the invisible furniture of someone else's turf or strongly held belief.

Television came into the picture about three months after my arrival in Washington, thanks to a partnership between the *Post* and MSNBC. That first invitation was as much about talking about the news of the day as it was an audition to see if I was "good TV." My relationship with MSNBC took off after a brief conversation with *Hardball* anchor Chris Matthews at an event at the Four Seasons Hotel in Georgetown.

The moderated panel on climate change with Tucker Carlson, Thomas Friedman, and Claire Shipman was my first big Washington event. The kind of event crowded with everyone you've ever seen on the Sunday shows. The Q&A period with the audience wasn't going well. Neither Teresa Heinz Kerry, who had a brand-new book out on the environment with her husband, Senator John Kerry; nor ABC News anchor George Stephanopoulos, who was sitting next to Tina Brown, the wife of the moderator, Sir Harold Evans; offered a question for the panel when prompted. Enter Chris Matthews.

"Chris, you must have a question," said Sir Harry, the famed author and journalist with whom I worked during his brief stint at the *New York Daily News*.

"Do I have a question? Yeah, I have a question," Matthews thundered from the table next to mine in the ballroom. "Where are the African Americans?" Evans appeared flummoxed.

"This is a majority African American city, and I'm looking at a panel filled with white faces!" Matthews continued.

The only other Black person at the event was seated clear across the ballroom. Our eyes locked, and all I could think was "WOW! This is GREAT!"

Evans countered, "Well, Chris, how many African Americans do you have on your show?!" Without missing a beat, Matthews leaned forward and yelled, "Not enough! We're always looking for African Americans to put on my show!"

Matthews was still a little hot when I went over to him after the event to tell him that I thought what he did was incredible. "I go to these events all the time, and I always see the same old white faces," he huffed. "And for him to make that crack about me and my show. I'm always looking for African Americans to put on my show!"

With that opening, I reached into my pocket and handed him my newly printed *Washington Post* business card. "Put me on your show," I said. He inquired what I did at the paper and asked me to send him my résumé. Declaring he had no card to offer in return, Chris gave me his email address. I sent what he requested that night.

About a week later, I was cc'd on an email from Matthews to his executive producer. The one and only Tammy Haddad, who was the senior producer of the *Today* show when I worked there as a researcher two years out of college. His message was something like "Impressive guy. Get him on the show." The next week began what would become weekly appearances on *Hardball*, which morphed into a near-daily presence on MSNBC.

A little more than a year later, I was in a diner in Denver for the 2008 Democratic National Convention. We'd just finished doing *Morning Joe*, then a year-old MSNBC show that had already become must-see TV for political junkies, when the show's creator and anchor, Joe Scarborough, asked if I was under contract yet. Nope.

So he yells, "Hey, Phil! We better sign Capehart before someone else does." Phil was Phil Griffin, the president of MSNBC, who was the hard-charging political producer I worked with when I was an intern on the *Today* show. By then, I already had a television contract with ABC's *This Week with George Stephanopoulos* to appear on their political roundtable. But Phil said that was fine. Promising to sign me on as an MSNBC contributor after we left Denver, Phil told me not to do any other cable networks, not Fox, not CNN, where I was making lots of appearances. I signed my first MSNBC contributor contract in 2009.

As much as I liked editorial writing, I loved writing under my own name. I wrote the occasional column in the newspaper, but it wasn't until the 2008 political conventions that I was given an outlet to write in my own voice. It liberated me from the relatively bland institutional voice required of editorial writing and gave me more freedom. I also could write in the colorful ways ingrained in me at the *New York Daily News*.

Sometime in early 2009, Fred asked me to write under my own name for the *Post Partisan* blog. That meant no more editorial writing, but I could stay on the editorial board, which was important to me.

The timing of this move could not have been better. The nation's first Black president had just been inaugurated and I was perfectly positioned to chronicle his historic time in the White House. In presence and rhetoric, people want to see themselves reflected in some way in their elected officials. President Barack Obama and his family represented the best of African American life. How they navigated the presidential campaign was a direct reflection of how I and millions of Black folks lived our lives and navigated a predominately white world.

At the *Daily News* and at Bloomberg News, I had brought my whole self to my column writing. And I continued doing that at the *Washington Post*. Since I was an out gay man and an African American, the Obama years gave me plenty of material to work with. The pride with which I performed my job in those years is incalculable. Whenever I did a television appearance, I made sure to do it from Pebble Beach, the bank of television cameras that positioned the White House perfectly behind correspondents reporting from the North Lawn. I made sure to call him "President Obama" to give him the respect many in the media and politics were refusing to give him.

Most importantly, in my columns, I found myself trying to explain and decode the Black man in the Oval Office. For white people, it was revealing why he would never show the flashes of anger they were used to from a commander in chief. For Black people, it was clarifying his reluctance to talk about race in public. The perils of which were on full display at the end of a July 2009 press conference when he was asked about the actions of the police in Cambridge, Massachusetts, in their arrest of Henry Louis Gates. Someone called the cops on the Black Harvard professor, who was locked out of his home and was trying to get in. Obama's comment that the police "acted stupidly" was no big deal to African Americans. But it enraged white folks. So much so that in his post-presidency memoir, Obama noted that his support among white voters plummeted after that comment and never fully recovered.

But in my columns at the *Post*, I also found myself decoding Black people for my white readers. And in this regard, the killing of Trayvon Martin was a defining moment for me. The seventeen-year-old's death in Sanford, Florida, at the hands of an overzealous neighborhood watch volunteer in 2012 tugged at my soul like no other beating or killing of an unarmed Black man had.

All he was doing was walking back to his father's girlfriend's house after going to a nearby convenience store. Skittles and iced tea were his purchases. Rain was coming down. His hoodie was up, a cell phone pressed to his ear as he talked to a friend. All the while, George Zimmerman was on the phone with 911 telling the operator, "We've had some break-ins in my neighborhood and there's a real suspicious guy. This guy looks like he's up to no good or he's on drugs or something."

Trayvon Martin was a typical American teenager with typical American teenager issues that I had somehow escaped. But his parents, when they came in for an editorial board meeting at the *Post* a month after their son's killing, reminded me so much of my own family. Tracy Martin is his generation's version of my Uncle McKinley Branch. Sybrina Fulton is very much like my Aunt Annie, McKinley's wife. Hardworking, salt-of-the-earth people who strove to expose Trayvon to the wider world's possibilities. Just like Annie and McKinley did for their son, Justin. Still, Trayvon was robbed of the benefit of the doubt in life and then was robbed of his humanity in death as people looked for ways to justify his killing.

I poured out my soul in countless columns about the case and about the impact it was having on African Americans. Leaning into my lifelong role as ambassador for the race for readers who might not actually know anyone Black or might not know what their Black friends or colleagues go through behind closed doors. The conversations that go on. The warnings issued. The worries that ripple through the home until a loved one returns or reaches their destination.

That swirl of terrified excitement at the *Post* had curdled into confusion and dread. An anxious state that resulted in a panic attack on an Amtrak train in 2012.

The Acela from Washington to New York was pulling out of the Baltimore station. I had just finished talking with Donna Brazile. The veteran Democratic political operative who managed Vice President Al Gore's 2000 presidential campaign—

the first Black woman to manage a major-party campaign— got off at that station and was walking by my window in a fabulous orange coat that billowed dramatically behind her when I was hit in the chest with a feeling so intense, I audibly gasped and grabbed at my shirt. My heart raced wildly. At the suggestion of my old New York doctor's office, I told the conductor what was happening and that I should get off the train at Wilmington. A forty-five-minute stretch that felt like an eternity for me and the first-class car attendant who sat with me.

The paramedics and police were waiting on the platform when the train pulled into Wilmington station. Nick drove up from Washington. The first time I told him I loved him was from the train as I feared the worst. My mother drove up from her home in Maryland. Refusing a hotel room of her own, she slept at the end of my bed during my one-night hospital stay. There was nothing physically wrong with me. All of my tests revealed a clean bill of health.

As a result of all this, I got a terrific new general practitioner who listened to me at length. Her diagnosis was immediate. I had suffered a panic attack, and she encouraged me to dig deep to understand what triggered it. I already knew the answer. The panic attack hit on February 10. The fifth anniversary of my move to Washington from New York. I missed the city. More importantly, I felt like I was on an island on my own within the Opinions section.

My writing got more emphatic with each successive killing of an unarmed Black person by police or vigilante. My own sense of security eroded with every incident to the point where I never left home without my driver's license, insurance card, and *Washington Post* business card with Nick's cell phone number on it as an "in case of emergency" contact. Each death was a reminder that one of the burdens of being a Black male is carrying the heavy weight of other people's suspicions. I was writing to inform as much as I was releasing my own fears. My columns on the killing of Michael Brown two years after the killing of Trayvon were no less emphatic. But that case later presented a professional and moral dilemma for me.

On August 9, 2014, a white police officer named Darren Wilson shot and killed Michael Brown, an unarmed Black eighteen-year-old walking with a friend in Ferguson, Missouri, a suburb outside of St. Louis. An eyewitness told the *St. Louis Post-Dispatch* "that she saw Brown trying to run away with his hands in the air before shots rang out." A rallying cry was born: "Hands up, don't shoot" was chanted in demonstrations across the country.

Just as with the killing of Trayvon Martin, I dove in. I linked Brown's killing to the others that had terrified Black America and enraged the nation. I wrote about everything from the demonstrations to the militarized response of the Missouri National Guard to the investigations and their aftermath. But seven months after Brown's killing, when the Justice Department released the blockbuster results of its two investigations, only one of them got attention.

The report on the Ferguson Police Department was 102 damning pages that detailed years of mistreatment by the police, the courts, and the municipal government, including evidence that all three balanced their books on the backs of the Black and poor people of Ferguson through traffic tickets, court fees, and other fines and fees.

Unlike the report on the Ferguson Police Department, I'd neither read nor talked about the Justice Department report on the shooting of Michael Brown. I moved to change that, and what I found in the 86-page "DOJ Report on Shooting of Michael Brown" made me ill.

The hands-up storyline wasn't corroborated by ballistic and DNA evidence and multiple witness statements. The new information, the new facts revealed that I had gotten the story wrong. The more I read, the more I felt compelled to correct the record, my record. What's more, this damning report was commissioned and approved by Eric Holder, the nation's first Black chief law enforcement officer, serving in the administration of the first Black president. The same Black man who rightly bemoaned that we were "a nation of cowards" when it came to race. As I kept reading, one question rolled through my head as if on an infinity loop: If I don't correct the record knowing what I know now, why would anyone trust me the next time there's a shooting of another unarmed Black person? (And I knew there would *always* be a next time.)

For almost a solid week, I wrote what I had learned. My usual process went into overdrive as I wrote the hardest piece I ever had to write. But my overarching mindset was the one that guided us during the Apollo Theater series. Let the facts do the talking. But this wasn't just a writing process, this was an emotional exercise. From battling in the 1990s with members of the LGBTQ+ community over gay sex clubs to brawling with the Black powerbrokers of Harlem over the Apollo, I knew from experience what it's like to take on a sacred cow. I knew that swinging a sledgehammer at an established narrative like "Hands up, don't shoot" was not going to be popular, that I was going to face backlash.

Maybe that's why I gave my column a bland headline: "Lesson Learned from the Shooting of Michael Brown." I had already gotten used to people popping off about the headlines of pieces they hadn't read. The initial headline was guaranteed to generate zero attention, which was why Jim Downie, my editor at the time, emailed to ask about changing it.

"Jonathan, is it alright if we tweak the headline on this? I think we'll get even better clickthroughs if the headline says what you've decided you got wrong. ('Justice Dept. report shows "Hands up, don't shoot" was built on a lie' or something like that.)," he wrote. He was right, so I wrote back, "hmmmm........ how about just: 'Hands up, don't shoot' was built on a lie." The piece and an accompanying video I did caused one of the most bizarre firestorms of my career.

The next day, during an interview with NPR, Melissa Block asked me about the criticism. I was being slammed by some on the right for being late to my conclusions. They were crowing that they knew all along that "Hands up, don't shoot" was a lie and were using the DOJ report to continue discounting the very real rage and fear that fueled the demonstrations. Meanwhile, African Americans were enraged. They said I had sold out. Block read one comment that was typical: "Hands up was more than Mike Brown. You just demeaned this child to be accepted by white people." That night, I watched in slack-jawed amazement as then–Fox News anchor Megyn Kelly and media critic Howie Kurtz devoted an entire segment to what I'd written. Kelly commended me for being "brave enough to admit he was wrong." The next day, Rupert Murdock's *New York Post* ran a story online.

My in-box and Twitter feed were soon flooded with messages from whites and conservatives congratulating me on my bravery, calling me "a real journalist" and "one of the good ones." Meanwhile, Blacks and progressives were ripping me to shreds. I was guilty of playing "respectability politics" to win white approval. I was an Uncle Tom, a house nigger. I was a traitor to the race. I would be lying if I said the barbs didn't sting in some way. They did. But I'd heard it all before in my life and career.

When columnist openings appeared on the op-ed page, I always made it known to Fred that I wanted to be considered. I had the experience. But each time, I got a polite hearing. Each time, I was passed over. The first few times, there was no announcement. I just happened to notice the new bylines on the page. Once Fred started announcing the hiring of new columnists with space in the paper and blogs named for them at the board meetings, I had to learn how to keep the disappointment from gnarling my usually expressive face, especially when the new hire was yet another one of our talented former summer interns.

This was another source of anxiety for me—invisibility where it mattered—and it wasn't new. Indeed, I had called Fred from the train as it sped to Wilmington. As someone who had a heart condition, he took my medical emergency very seriously. We met in his office on my first day back at the paper. It just so happened to be my fifth anniversary at the *Post*. I told him that what had triggered my panic attack was my situation at the paper. Feeling like I was doing a lot and getting no recognition or even feedback in return. How being passed over for a columnist spot multiple times without so much as a "thanks, but no thanks" only added to the gnawing sense that I didn't belong, that my contributions weren't valued. "I don't like feeling like I'm just taking up space," I told him.

Fred assured me that wasn't the case. That I was a valued member of the board and the section. This ebb and flow between my feeling undervalued and Fred reassuring me that wasn't the case would come to characterize our complicated relationship. An exhausting pattern over the years that led me to seek advice on how to cope with it, on whether I should leave the *Post*. So I sent a bat signal to the one person who would have just the perspective I needed.

Gwen Ifill was a living legend. A no-nonsense journalist whose storied career took her from the *Washington Post* to the *New York Times* to NBC to PBS. She became the first Black woman to host a national television political talk show when she took the helm of *Washington Week* on PBS in 1999. She appeared on the Sunday shows and moderated the 2004 and 2008 vice presidential debates. And she was revered by her friends. Gwen was the mistress of tough love with an emphasis on love. She told you what you needed to hear because she loved you enough to tell you.

Over breakfast at the Fairmont Hotel in 2014, Gwen listened as I unspooled years of frustration. Having worked at the *Post*, she understood the culture of the place and its people. She peppered me with questions about the work I was doing. She probed what exactly I wanted to happen. Then, after telling me not to quit a job without having a new one, something I assured her would not happen "because I'm a Black man in America," Gwen delivered a piece of advice that became an instant life lesson.

"Make it work for you, because that's what they would do," Gwen said.

Who "they" were was clear: my white colleagues. They are adept at turning lemons into lemonade, making whatever imperfect situation work for them. But the key piece of her advice was to make it work for *me*. It took me a little while to figure out what that would look like, but when I did, I said yes to invitations that allowed me to go where my talents were wanted.

You want me to guest-host *The Leonard Lopate Show* on WNYC for a week? You bet. You want me to substitute-anchor a show on MSNBC from New York? Absolutely. You want me to moderate a panel in Marrakesh? Sure thing. For years, my conference rotation included the Aspen Ideas Festival in Colorado in June; NYU's La Pietra Dialogues in Florence, Italy, in October or November; the Atlantic Dialogues conference hosted by the German Marshall Fund in Marrakech, Morocco, in December; and the Brussels Forum in Belgium in March. With lots of others in between.

The idea of my *Cape Up* podcast had grown out of a live twenty-minute interview I did with Eric Holder when he was attorney general of the United States as part of the *Atlantic* magazine's Washington Ideas Forum in 2014. Those podcast sit-downs helped me refine my skills as an interviewer. And I discovered a love of doing live events by doing more of them for organizations such as the 92nd Street Y in New York, Sixth & I in Washington, and Connecticut Forum or the nearly sold-out *Promise Me, Dad* book event I did with then–private citizen Joe Biden at the 2,600-seat Proctors Theater in Schenectady, New York.

I went wherever my talents were wanted, oftentimes at my own expense. But I was compelled to do so because I believed something very strongly, a belief that took root in my later years in New York: Everything we do in life is an audition for something. We just don't know what for yet.

The *Wall Street Journal* exclusive story on June 24, 2020, was a TV biz thunderbolt. Joy Reid, anchor of MSNBC's popular weekend show *AM Joy*, was expected to be named the new host of the 7:00 p.m. slot vacated by Chris Matthews in a surprise on-air resignation three months earlier. That meant her chair on Saturdays and Sundays (10:00 a.m.–12:00 p.m.) would need to be filled. As a frequent substitute host for her, I wanted to go for it. I just needed to get into the audition rotation, which was going to be difficult because the rumor started circulating internally that the next host had to be a Black woman.

The ascension a month earlier of Cesar Conde as the new president of NBC Universal News Group turned out to be a blessed development. The Harvard-Wharton grad had been chairman of NBC Universal International Group and Telemundo Enterprises. He also served on the board of PepsiCo. Reading that nugget in his bio, I immediately texted Darren Walker, who also served on that board, to see if he would be willing to make an introduction. He did. And a Zoom meeting was set. In the days before our meeting, Cesar and I each discovered that we shared Alberto Ibargüen, then the president of the Knight Foundation, as a friend and mentor.

Cesar asked all the questions. He wanted to know about my childhood, where I went to college, how I got to NBC, my relationships within the network. I was moved by his curiosity and interest. At the end of the thirty-minute meeting, Cesar asked, "Where do you see yourself in five years?" When someone asks you what you want, tell them. So I told him.

"Of course, I'd love to have a show, but my ask of you today is to just give me a shot to audition for the *AM Joy* slot," I replied.

During the audition phase, I put all the skills I had learned and developed over years of podcast and radio interviews and live events to work on television. I also helped to book big guests for the shows I anchored. This was my one shot, and I wasn't going to waste it. Every day in the chair was an opportunity to show Cesar Conde, Phil Griffin, and Rashida Jones, the troika making the decision, that I could hold the chair, do the job.

After three months of Nick racing me up and down Interstate 95 to 30 Rock in the middle of the COVID pandemic, I got the call on October 30, 2020. As I sat in a hotel room high above Midtown Manhattan with the Empire State looming outside the window behind me, Phil told me I was getting a show, the Sunday show. Even though I didn't get both days, I was elated. I had dreamed of getting a call like that my entire life. I had prepared my entire life for the opportunity I was now given.

That call from Phil wasn't the only one opening a career-altering opportunity. Sara Just, executive producer of *PBS NewsHour*, called with a query. From time to time, I was asked to sit in for legendary Washington political columnist and commentator Mark Shields, the Shields of the popular "Shields and Brooks" segment on the Friday edition of *PBS NewsHour*. There are few segments in television journalism that have attained iconic status. "Shields and Brooks" was one of them. Shields held his spot in the segment for thirty-two years with different counterparts, including *New York Times* columnist David Brooks for the last nineteen of those years. Shields was revered by his colleagues and especially by the audience. Sara wanted to know if I would be interested in succeeding him after his retirement. I was floored. I was honored.

Looking at the shoes I would try to fill was akin to a little boy looking at his dad's wingtips. Stepping into them once the segment became "Brooks and Capehart" in January 2021 was daunting. The audience looks to me and David for clarity, direction, and certainly some validation. They are not shy about letting me know what they think of what I say. But the best comment to me came from Shields himself at a book party held at the home of *PBS NewsHour* anchor Judy Woodruff less than a month before he passed away.

"You're doing a great job," he told me as I held back tears.

By going to where my talents were wanted and making the exhausting ebb and flow at the *Post* work for me, as the great Gwen Ifill advised, I unwittingly built an incredible, multiplatform career. But there comes a time in one's career when you have to choose. When your principles and even your dignity are on the line. For the first time in my twenty-five years as a journalist, I was faced with such a choice. And what to do next came so quickly and naturally to mind that it felt automatic: resign from the editorial board.

CHAPTER 14

WHY I LEFT THE EDITORIAL BOARD

The 2022 midterm elections produced some surprises. The so-called red wave of Republicans into the House of Representatives never materialized. But a runoff in the Georgia Senate race between Democratic incumbent Senator Raphael Warnock and Herschel Walker, his Republican challenger, did materialize. A stunning battle between the senior pastor of the historic Ebenezer Baptist Church made famous by Martin Luther King Jr. and the former professional football player who won the Heisman Trophy in 1982.

Early voting in Georgia also proved surprising. In the aftermath of the 2020 presidential election, which saw Joe Biden win the state—the first Democrat to do so since Bill Clinton in 1992—the Georgia state legislature moved to restrict voting and even opened the possibility that not all votes cast might actually be counted. And yet, despite the numerous barriers that made exercising the franchise even more difficult, Georgians stood in line or cast ballots by mail in record numbers. This revelation led Karen Tumulty, the new leader of the board, to propose an editorial in praise of the early vote count so far and to slam President Biden for his characterization of the Georgia voting law as "Jim Crow 2.0."

In anticipation of Jackson Diehl's retirement in August 2021, Fred Hiatt chose Tumulty as his new deputy. A legendary political reporter, who has covered the White House, Congress, and presidential campaigns for nearly five decades, she came to the *Post* in 2010 and joined the Opinions section in 2018. She became the leader of the section when Fred suddenly passed away four months later, in December 2021.

"How could it be voter suppression if all these people are coming out to vote?" I recall Tumulty saying with a tone of amazement. There were some objections, including from me. Without a clear consensus, the idea of an editorial was dead.

The conversation at the meeting disturbed me. So much so that I penned an email to everyone who was at the meeting in person or via Zoom that fleshed out my thoughts. And then I turned it into a column that ran online on November 9.

"Voting should be as easy as possible and obstacles that get in the way of that are about trying to diminish some voters' ability to exercise the franchise," I wrote in the November 2 missive, pointing out that just because people clear the obstacles doesn't mean the obstacles are not a big deal. I then likened it to restrictions on abortion. "Roe set limits, but then some states set about putting up obstacles to women's ability to exercise

their constitutional right to an abortion: waiting periods, man-
dated counseling, fetal heartbeat bills, funding restrictions
that shut down clinics that provided abortion care and forced
women to drive hundreds of miles for such care, bans that
make abortion illegal at 10 weeks, 6 weeks or conception, etc.,"
I continued. "I'm happy for the women who have successfully
run that gauntlet to get the care she wanted/needed. But she
should not have had to jump through any or all those hoops to
get it. I'm happy Georgia voters are showing up in record numbers despite the post-2020 election restrictions and limitations
placed on their ability to vote. But they should not have needed
organizations like Fair Vote, Black Voters Matter and others to
help them overcome those restrictions or limitations on their
right to vote."

In the lead-up to the December 6 Georgia runoff election, there were discussions about the state of the race, the fact
that the race appeared close despite Walker's clear deficiencies,
and the move by the Democratic National Committee to shift
the Peach State's primary higher on the primary calendar. I don't
recall hearing anyone make the flawed "Jim Crow 2.0" argument
again. As the date got closer, there were conversations about the
editorial writer penning two different pieces. One for a Warnock
victory. One for a Walker victory. The polls were that maddeningly close.

As a member of the editorial board, I could have read the
editorial by going into the electronic basket in our system. That's
where all editorials are filed before publication and can be read
by anyone with access to it. Doing so gives you the chance to
express concerns or objections about anything in the piece to the
writer or directly to the editor. That's when issues can be resolved,

arguments can be won or lost one last time. But I didn't. Remember, editorials are consensus documents that express the collective view of those around the table. There were no warning signs. No red flags. Nothing alarming that would push me to ensure I look at what was going to go out from the board.

I was sitting at my desk in the den of my apartment when I read the editorial in the print edition on December 8. A fine, perfectly reasonable piece that lauded Warnock's win and the decision by the DNC to move up in the primary calendar the state Biden won in 2020 by 0.3 percentage points. Reasonable until I hit the third sentence of the fifth paragraph.

> And turnout remained high despite hyperbolic warnings by President Biden and other Democrats that updated voting rules amounted to Jim Crow 2.0.

I was a tornado of emotions, eye-popping rage, and disbelief. I couldn't stay.

The first time David Shipley and I spoke was by telephone in August 2022. The former chief of Bloomberg View had been tapped by *Post* publisher Fred Ryan the previous month to fill the void left by Fred Hiatt's sudden death eight months earlier. Shipley was making the rounds, getting to know the people who made up a still-grieving Opinions section. In that conversation, I told him I wanted to leave the editorial board, that fifteen years was long enough. I wanted off the board not only because it was time, but also because the dynamic no longer felt right.

For thirteen of those fifteen years, I had not written an editorial. And that was by design.

Sitting at the ed board table was very important to me. I was only one voice and didn't speak for all gay or all Black or all gay Black people. But I was the only one in that room, at that table. And when you are "the only one," the responsibility to be a voice for all those not there, not present, is a weight impossible to ignore. My being at the table was also important to Fred Hiatt. He understood the importance of having around that table a Black and gay perspective that would bring much-needed context to particular issues animating the national conversation, from the cultural importance of the Obama presidency to police-involved killings of unarmed African Americans to the fight for marriage equality. When I spoke on those issues and others related to race and LGBTQ+ matters, Fred listened. We didn't always agree on policy issues in those arenas, but I always felt heard. It was a grand bargain. One that became less and less tenable as the years wore on and impossible to maintain after Fred's passing.

That terrified excitement and panic that marked my early years at the *Post* curdled into resentment as I began to feel like no one really cared what I thought or what I was working on. I kept my remarks short and to the point in our meetings. Then, resentment slid into silence. I shared less and less. I showed up less and less. No one seemed to notice. But after reading that "Jim Crow 2.0" line, I knew my time as the Black face of the editorial board had to end immediately.

The afternoon of December 8, the day the editorial appeared in the print edition, I sent my resignation email to Shipley. I noted how the word "hyperbolic" rankled me because it ignored the arguments I made at the board meeting and in the email I sent to the board the same day. I pointed out that my more than two decades sitting on editorial boards in New York and Washington taught me that editorials are the result of internal debate and that had anyone engaged me further, I would at least have felt heard and maybe even accepted the ultimate position. Then, I got to the heart of why what happened was the last straw. For most of my fifteen years on the editorial board, I had the distinction of being the only African American at the table, including when we discussed early voting in Georgia. Also, under my picture online, my area of focus was listed as national politics.

"But on a national political issue of great importance to African Americans, I was not only ignored, but also my stance wasn't even acknowledged in private," I wrote. "While it is indeed an honor and a privilege to sit at our distinguished table, I can no longer abide what in recent years has come to feel more like an exercise in tokenism."

Shipley tried twice to convince me to stay on the editorial board. Both times I declined and explained why. How could I sit around a table with people who did something I viewed as a professional violation and a personal betrayal? In hindsight, it felt like it did when I broke the unspoken agreement with my white friends growing up. The one designed for maximum white comfort with my Black presence. I was no longer going to provide cover for folks who demonstrated quite clearly that my voice, my perspective, didn't matter.

Shipley accepted my decision and expressed regret over how it all happened. He then asked how I wanted to proceed. After a day or two of distance, I sent Tumulty and her deputy the same email I sent to Shipley, only with a different, valedictory ending.

I had to read Tumulty's response several times, because I couldn't believe what she wrote.

> Look forward to discussing. The word "hyperbolic" specifically referred to comparisons with Jim Crow, which I think is defensible.

To ensure that my feeling offended was not an overreaction, I shared her response with Nick and five other gut-check friends. I even talked to a fellow columnist, whose response was "What in the fucking actual fuck?!"

———

After a few failed attempts, Tumulty and I never did talk about it. Her deputy and I had a conversation the same day I sent the email. I will be forever grateful for his empathy and humanity during what was one of the most difficult periods of my professional career.

What I was going through was not as publicly humiliating as being screamed at by the head of Bloomberg News twenty years earlier. It was a private humiliation that forced me to contend with my loneliness in the Opinions section. A loneliness that was compounded by a searing hurt as I began to feel that my colleagues, many of whom I worked with for fifteen years, didn't give a damn. Sitting in my office brought back many of the panic attack symptoms I felt during that episode on the train a decade earlier. The racing heart and sweaty palms. The physical drain that comes with trying to get in the mental space needed to power through it to feel at peace, normal.

For years, among the people in the Opinions section, I often felt that I was the one whose face was continually pressed up against the glass. Glass that was opaque in some way. I couldn't see what was happening on the other side, but I could hear fragments of conversations about dinners or tennis or some excursion. Conversations that let me know there was a community on the other side of that glass that I wasn't invited to join.

A month had gone by when a board member and I ran into each other at the coffee joint in the lobby. Something he said made me ask him if he knew I'd left the board. He didn't know. He hadn't a clue.

Tired of feeling trapped by a sense of indifference, I went to the head of HR. Wayne has the calm and focused demeanor of a therapist. Or a divinity student who opted to forgo the priesthood. He possesses a real-life poker face that registers nothing. Neither judgment, nor approval. His questions were probing. My answers waded deep into my feelings of alienation, my challenging relationship with the section in general, and what I wanted to come out of all this. First and foremost, I wanted the board to be told that I had stepped down.

Wayne asked if I minded if he talked with Shipley and Tumulty. Of course not, I said. The result was a meeting between me and Shipley where he asked what I wanted. I told him I simply wanted the board told I had stepped aside. I wanted my departure acknowledged. I wanted my fifteen years to count for something. Shipley told the board the next day.

The email from Tumulty asking to meet struck me as another indication that she didn't fully grasp the severity of the situation. "Sounds like there have been multiple misunderstandings," she wrote. "Would love to have the talk we never got to have."

I was sitting in my office when Tumulty appeared. Taking one of the guest chairs, she folded her arms and began her apology. "There have been multiple misunderstandings or whatever," she began. She then said, "I'm sorry." I don't recall the words immediately after that because of what came in the next breath. "But I do think use of the word 'hyperbolic' is defensible." In that moment, I thought for sure I was being punked. But that wasn't even the worst of it. Tumulty then made a pronouncement.

"I have a rule: No one should be called a Nazi unless they were an actual Nazi," she told me. "So for President Biden to call the Georgia voter law 'Jim Crow 2.0,' well that's an insult to people who lived through Jim Crow."

I sat frozen, gripping the armrests of my chair as I stared at her in disbelief. With that one comment, Tumulty took an incident where I felt ignored and compounded the insult by robbing me of my humanity. She either couldn't or wouldn't see that I was Black, that I came to the conversation with knowledge and history she could never have, that my worldview, albeit different from hers, was equally valid.

In situations like this, Black professionals have a different kind of fight-or-flight response. Flight, meaning to ignore the offense and put distance between you and the offender going forward. Fight, meaning to engage the offense or the offender, to lay down a marker that you are not one to be belittled, diminished, or dismissed. I chose the latter.

"President Biden didn't make up the phrase 'Jim Crow 2.0.' African Americans have been saying it for years," I interjected, noting that it's called "Jim Crow 2.0" because Jim Crow morphs. Its contours and shapes change depending on the suppression needed to keep Black people from exercising rights guaranteed to all Americans under the Constitution.

Our conversation began to resemble tires on an icy road, circling fast and going nowhere. Tumulty declared we were talking past each other. An assessment I agreed with just to bring the conversation to an end. We weren't talking past each other. I didn't think she was listening. I then tried to impress upon her that the issue that brought us together was bigger than one word or phrase in an editorial. I told her that what happened was painful and insulting. But it seemed to me that Tumulty didn't fully appreciate why. So I delivered a blunt assessment. "Karen, you have a giant blind spot that is going to put you, the board, the page, the section, and quite possibly the paper in danger."

She later asked if we could hit refresh on things and start anew. My voice said, "We can try." My face said, "Get the hell out of my office!"

I sat in stunned, unblinking silence for what seemed like ten minutes after Tumulty removed herself from my office. My mind reeled with what had just happened. In a time when people, especially white people, are so careful not to make racial situations worse, Tumulty seemed to have done just that.

My notebook ever at the ready, I wrote down what I could remember from what had just happened and used those notes to fire off an email to Wayne in HR and to Shipley, whose face was a little red when we met the next day. His eyes looked like two big, wet marbles as he said, "I'm so sorry you're going through this."

For months, going to my office at the *Post* filled me with dread. I feared running into Tumulty and the emotions it unleashed. In fact, I didn't want to see any of my colleagues. Then again, they didn't really see me. Not even two months later when Axios broke the story of my departure from the board and the circumstances that led to it. No one reached out to get my side of the story or even check to see if I was okay. It was like I was Bruce Willis in the closing minutes of *The Sixth Sense* and I was finally realizing I was dead.

I talked to a few friends in confidence about what was going on. They listened. They gave advice. A couple of friends even said, "You can't stay there." Another friend called me out of the blue on Super Bowl Sunday. Just to say hi. As we caught up, I struggled with whether to tell her what I was going through. But I gave in. I needed to tell her if only to unburden myself of the stress and sadness that had swamped my spirit. She then gave me a lengthy pep talk that left me in tears. Happy, relieved tears.

She told me I shouldn't suffer alone and urged me to go public "because it's not just about you." I knew what she meant. I may have sat at that ed board table as "the only one," but I wasn't alone. I brought a community with me. My seat at that table gave the community a voice at that table. "You'll be doing a disservice" by staying silent, she said.

Ultimately, I decided to wait to tell this story until now. I needed time and emotional distance to process what I went through. I'm not unique in what I experienced. Black people up and down the socioeconomic ladder go through some form of it daily. No one is exempt, no matter how high on the ladder they are or might seem. But what I experienced was uniquely painful for me, given my job and how I viewed my role in it. I had the ultimate job for a kid who once fancied himself an ambassador for the race, an interlocutor between Blacks and whites. And once again, it felt like the whiter world let me know where it believed my place to be.

Seven months after the whole mess started, an email hit my in-box that felt like a balm and for me personally a form of justice. In a series of staff announcements, Shipley informed us, "Karen has decided to step down as head of the editorial board and return to full-time columnizing."

CHAPTER 15

NICK

Dressed in matching navy blue tuxedos, Nick and I stood on a little riser in the Book Room of the Jefferson Hotel. This jewel just up 16th Street from the White House was where I stayed in the early 2000s when I worked at Bloomberg News and would come to Washington to try to get to know it the way I knew New York. Less than ten years later, the elegant hotel's newly renovated Quill Bar with its chic orange resin bar would become my go-to getaway for a quiet lunch or uncrowded drinks and dinner when I moved to town. And when Nick and I became a couple, he gladly accepted it as a member of our restaurant rotation. Those tried-and-true places that feel like home without having to do the dishes. The Jefferson was home.

In four short weeks, we went from the idea of moving up our wedding date to standing before a small group of friends who came from Los Angeles and the Bay Area and New York. In retrospect, given the guest list and the continued state of disbelief from the election, we shouldn't have been surprised that of the forty people we invited, thirty-nine of them accepted. Nick's father had just had knee replacement surgery and couldn't fly. Valerie Jarrett looked beautiful in her fuchsia jacket topped with a colorful wrap that made everything pop. Of all the people in attendance, it was imperative that the senior adviser to President Obama be there. Getting to this day was all her doing.

In the kitchen of Robert Raben, a Justice Department official in the Clinton administration who hung out his own shingle in 2001 to create one of the most prominent progressive public affairs shops in Washington, was where it happened. "When are you getting married?" Valerie asked me, as was her wont in the months after the *Obergefell* decision.

Valerie's only ten years older than me, but she has the wisdom of an elder many more years my senior. She is that stylish cousin you can't wait to show up at a family gathering because she inspires you to be and do your best while mixing in some good-natured teasing. You can't wait to talk to her, even if the conversation veers to the uncomfortable. I tried to laugh off her latest inquiry, which became my default response to that feared question that had hounded straight people for millennia.

"C'mon, Valerie," I laughed, rolling my eyes in exaggerated exasperation as I looked away.

"Jonathan, what's the problem? What's going on?" she persisted, her eyes fixed on me.

"I'm going to tell you what the president tells the young, straight guys who are on his staff and in relationships," Valerie continued. "He asks them two questions. The first question he asks is 'Do you love her?' The next is, 'Do you know for a fact she wants to marry you?' If the answer to both those questions is yes, then you have to get married. If you don't want to, then you should end the relationship. It's not fair to her." That last point made all the more important because of the biological clock. Something neither Nick nor I had.

"So," Valerie pressed. "Do you love him?"

"Yes," I said, now avoiding her eyes by looking at the bottles of wine arrayed before me.

"Do you know for a fact he wants to marry you?" she asked.

"Yes," I said with a heavy sigh and another roll of the eyes. "He's been dropping hints for months now."

In all honesty, I wasn't ready standing there in Robert's kitchen under Valerie's unflinching "you know I'm right" gaze. None of my excuses passed muster with her.

"When you find the right person, why wait?" Valerie said before her attention turned to new arrivals.

The conversation was short and exhausting. The impact was enduring. In the dawn of a morning in the days after talking to Valerie, I found myself staring at a still-slumbering Nick. There was a third question that I hadn't allowed myself to consider, let alone answer. Did I want to marry him? As I looked at his face, covered in a light moss of red stubble, I thought, "Yeah!"

And then, over the next four months, I set about secretly planning the proposal. I was already planning a summer vacation for us in southern Italy, so when I saw the blue-tiled roof terrace of Torre Trasita in Positano, a spectacular Airbnb that looks like a castle tower dangled over the Mediterranean, I knew it was the perfect place to change our life together. Four months of secret planning and a case of vertigo later, I did it.

Despite taking an Ambien before going to bed on our first night in Italy, we both awoke just after the first light started streaking across the morning sky. The sun still had not crested the high rolling mountains of the Amalfi Coast when we made our way up to the terrace and I plotted the where and the when of the big moment. Then I took my leave of the terrace to get everything.

The handwritten proposal that I had drafted and futzed with every day over those months was sealed in its envelope and placed in my ubiquitous Moleskine notebook. The engagement ring was back in its red leather Cartier box after making its way undetected from its secret hiding spot in Washington to my carry-on luggage to the pocket of the sweatpants I wore. When Nick went back downstairs and inside to make coffee, I raced about the terrace scouting out various places until I settled on a spot. The two precious parcels were propped up on a wrought iron fixture on the terrace wall. The absence of wind kept the proposal from blowing into the sea. The waiting for Nick to return slowly driving me mad.

Upon his return, Nick greeted me with the same question he always asks when he's been away from me for longer than five minutes. "What are you doing, Groover?" he said, employing his nickname for me ever since a trip to Los Angeles a few years back. A response to his daily query on this particular moment was the one thing I didn't plan for. I expected him to see the red box. I expected him to save me from talking. That was what the card was for. So I said the first thing that came to mind.

"I'm waiting for you to look at what Santa Claus brought you," I said, sitting inches away from what Nick didn't see. It was an odd thing to say, especially because it was late May. Understandably confused, Nick said, "What?"

Through gritted teeth and with my index finger thrusting toward the impromptu display, I said, with exasperation because I was about to be consumed by my own anxiety, "Just look at what Santa Claus brought you!"

He opened the envelope addressed to "Magoo," my nickname given to him on that same Los Angeles trip and read the handwritten note. His face darted up and eyes immediately looked at me after reading the words "Marry me." The series of photos I took during all this show that Nick didn't fully grasp what was happening until he saw the engagement ring. His say-what-now expression after reading the proposal giving way to joy. Between the surprise and the Ambien haze, Nick didn't say yes until I asked him panicked, "Well, what's your answer?"

Before I met Nick Schmit, I pretty much kept to myself. I went to work. I went to dinner at one of my haunts and then I went home. I only did things with friends. Movies, dinner, brunch. I went for early morning runs on the weekends. I dated a bunch but fell into my pattern of falling for guys too quickly or falling for guys who were not available or both.

Then, I was introduced to Nick.

Jed Hastings and his husband, Joe Solmonese, then the president of the Human Rights Campaign, were friends. Jed sent me a message on Facebook in November 2010 asking if I was dating because he wanted me to meet his cousin. Really his cousin by marriage since Nick's cousin is married to Jed's brother. I wanted to see what he looked like. What Jed sent was a photo of a cute young man, a handsomer version of Conan O'Brien with equally beautiful red hair. I was game.

Since Nick was traveling in Japan for the State Department, Jed told me to follow him on Facebook and to message him. You can tell a lot about someone by how they write. Nothing was sexier to me than good grammar and a perfectly placed comma. Nick wrote well. Instant messaging on Facebook moved to email and then moved to texting. A date was set.

Nick declined my offer to pick him up for our dinner at Buck's Fishing & Camping, a swell restaurant with a fabulous burger and chocolate cake. Instead, he said he would meet me at the Cleveland Park metro station. I suggested we meet at the gas station across the street on Connecticut Avenue since I had to fill up anyway. There, as I held the nozzle in place, I watched the traffic and people go by in the early-evening darkness, eagerly awaiting Nick's arrival. Like he was a latter-day Miss Betsy, the wonderful white woman who was my grandmother's Jehovah's Witnesses sidekick, popping out of her nighttime hiding spot to hop in the car.

Dinner was nice, but we both played it very cool. I especially so. Far too many times had I gone on a first date with a handsome, interesting man and started setting expectations and life goals before the entrées hit the table. If there were subsequent dates, the romance invariably fizzled in Goldilocks fashion. One fella was too "this." Another fella was too "that." Or I was that for them. "Just right" proved elusive.

We didn't play it so cool that we didn't agree to another date. Because Thanksgiving was the following week and then he was off to Hawaii for four weeks for work, we had our second date two nights later at Hank's Oyster Bar, around the corner from my apartment. He drove himself this time. This date was much better. We both let our guards down. Nick was funny and charming with his deadpanned jokes that still leave me wondering if he's being serious.

He told me about his two older sisters, Sara and Tina, and their children, and his younger brother David, who he calls Kenny. How he was Nicholas IV, named after his father, grandfather (a World War II veteran and proud Democrat who once served in the North Dakota State Senate), and great-grandfather (who emigrated from Luxembourg to the United States in 1908 when he was just sixteen years old). And that the family was in the house-moving business.

Since 1936, Schmit Movers transferred all kinds of structures from one location to another all over North Dakota and Minnesota. Entire houses, buildings, barns, churches, and the like. The Schmits were not unfamiliar to me. They sounded like the hardworking Minnesotans I knew while at Carleton. Nick told me how a college semester abroad changed the trajectory of his life. How it had led him to an internship at the Clinton Foundation in Harlem, which saw him becoming director of finance and administration before moving to Washington in 2007 to work on then-Senator Hillary Clinton's 2008 presidential campaign. Over dinner, we discovered that we had been in some of the same spaces in New York City, probably at the same time. I, in turn, told Nick about my North Carolina summers and the family barbecue my mother organized every year. We had a good time.

I walked Nick to his car. There, on the sidewalk, came that awkward "what do we do now" moment. We both said we had a nice time and would like to see each other again. But he was going away for such a long time. "Well, see you in 2014," I joked before we shared a tender kiss under the harsh glare of a DC streetlamp. And that's how our story began. We emailed while Nick was away, and upon his return, we picked up where we'd left off. After years of "crazy flings" that were "too hot not to cool down," my relationship with Nick developed slowly. Just like a nice winter fire, you can't hurry love.

Nick was frantically hashing out ancestral lines on a piece of paper as the plane was making its final descent into Fargo, North Dakota. An array of aunts and uncles, brothers and sisters, nieces and nephews, and a plethora of cousins impossible to remember in those fleeting moments before I was to meet a smiling Mrs. Schmit. I was going to be meeting all of these people at a family gathering at the home of Nick's Uncle Tony and Aunt Vonnie on Ottertail Lake, Minnesota.

This was a huge moment for Nick, who is called Nicholas by his family. A literal coming-out party for the third child of Nick and Jan Schmit. Not only that, but he was also bringing someone special home. While Nicholas's mother had long known he was gay, his father did not. Not until the two talked by phone a week before our arrival. The elder Nick was driving between house-moving jobs in North Dakota when it happened. The conversation was brief. Nick is not one for small talk. But it went much better than Nicholas had expected.

Our debut was a triumph. Excitement was in the air when we arrived at Tony and Vonnie's. An excitement you can see in the setting-sun-dappled family photo we took. I was the one on the far left. The Black dot in a sea of Midwestern white.

Everyone's warm embrace of us and me in particular pleasantly surprised us. Tony and Vonnie ensured I felt at home. They adored their nephew. And before Nick and I returned to Washington, his mother pulled me aside to express her happiness. "I've never seen him so happy," she said of her son.

Because of his travel schedule, the first two years of our relationship were spent mostly apart. Not that I minded. I was happy to be off the market and focused on one person. But that didn't mean there weren't moments of personal terror about the implications of various decisions. I knew I was all in the moment I gave Nick the extra set of keys to my apartment. Before, I used to buzz him up using a burner cell phone purchased for that sole purpose. That function only worked with cell phones with a (202) area code, and I wasn't about to give up my (917) number. That and my Century Association membership are the only things I own of New York City. Yet I tired of having to go downstairs to let the cutie in.

After what seemed like weeks of internal debate, I gave him the keys, thinking it would be a convenience for me when he visited. The very next day, I was overnighting in New York for MSNBC duty. When I texted Nick our customary "whachadoin'?" query, he wrote back, "Watching TV." Then came the picture. His feet on my sofa with the television on in the background. He never left.

Nick and I were starting to plan a different future in the run-up to the November 2016 elections. A Hillary Clinton victory would have opened a world of opportunity for my fiancé. At the request of the transition, Nick submitted five positions he was interested in. Moving to Europe was in the mix. But history had a different plan. Nick was under the unshattered glass of the Javits

Center on Manhattan's far West Side, and I was nestled into a bottle of red wine, flipping between MSNBC and CNN on the sofa at home in Washington as the certainty of a Clinton victory gave way to the reality that Donald Trump had been elected the 45th President of the United States.

More than a year earlier, Nick and I were among the thousands drawn to Lafayette Park to bear witness to the ultimate expression of our nation's embrace of liberty for all. On June 26, 2015, as night took over the evening sky, the White House was aglow in the colors of the rainbow to celebrate the Supreme Court ruling in *Obergefell v. Hodges*, a 5–4 decision that guaranteed the constitutional right to marry for same-sex couples. What made the experience more sublime and moving for me was knowing who was responsible for such a stirring demonstration of equality, of unity.

As a Black man and as a gay man, my two identities, often in conflict with each other and outside forces, found a home in the Oval Office of President Obama. His campaigns and two terms in office as the nation's first African American commander-in-chief were a direct reflection of how I have had to live my life as a Black professional. Navigating race in predominantly white spaces is a skill honed over years of interaction filled with a maddening mix of peril and promise that yields rewards for the most capable, but not without pain. His embrace of my humanity as a gay man, his championing of the rights of LGBTQ+ Americans to fully participate in our grand democratic experiment, made me feel wholly and proudly American.

I love America. That warm June night, America loved me back. But ten days earlier, a different tone was struck in the gaudy lobby of a Fifth Avenue tower that proved to be an omen.

"When Mexico sends its people, they're not sending their best," Trump said after descending an escalator to the marble floor of his eponymous tower, where he lived and worked. "They're sending people that have lots of problems, and they're bringing those problems with them. They're bringing drugs. They're bringing crime. They're rapists. And some, I assume, are good people." Seeing his poll numbers steadily rise with each insult and offense, Trump continued to play on base fears. He insisted on scratching at America's unhealed wounds and was rewarded for it.

Our wedding was set to take place on November 4, 2017, at Meridian International Center, perched atop a hill off 16th Street and across from Meridian Hill Park (or Malcolm X Park as it is known by Black DC). The White-Meyer House, one of the two grand houses that make up the august campus, was where Katharine Graham, the late publisher of the *Washington Post*, lived with her parents as a teen. We'd spent a lot of time at Meridian House, the site of many events, including the Meridian Ball, where official Washington and the diplomatic corps come together on an October night after dining in black tie at embassies around the city. Getting married there would have allowed us to have a large ceremony with dinner and dancing under one roof. The decision to scuttle those plans was sudden.

Someone quipped to us that we should get hitched before Trump swooped in and took gay marriage away. Nick and I looked at each other and said, "Yeah!" Not because of Trump. Because of Obama. The more we talked about it, the more we wanted to be married while he was still president, our president. I told him as much in the twenty seconds Nick and I had with him and First Lady Michelle Obama as we had our photo taken with them at one of their last holiday parties in the White House. The question was who was going to officiate.

During his time as attorney general, Eric Holder was regarded as Obama's ideological twin. The two men were introduced before the 2008 presidential campaign, and once in office, Holder was believed to give life to Obama's inner thoughts. The attorney general could say the things the president couldn't or wouldn't say, particularly on matters of race. Yet it was Holder's words and actions on same-sex marriage that made him the perfect person to marry us.

The road to marriage equality was long and bumpy. The so-called Defense of Marriage Act of 1996 was a mean-spirited roadblock that denied committed same-sex couples the rights and responsibilities that accrue to marriage. There were many court challenges, but *United States v. Windsor* was the case that forced the Supreme Court to confront the question of DOMA's constitutionality as it applied to same-sex couples legally married in the states where they lived. Tony West was the associate attorney general of the United States in charge of the Civil Rights Division when he led the interagency process that resulted in him urging the Justice Department to no longer defend DOMA in court because it was unconstitutional. Holder agreed.

Same-sex marriage was legal in only six states when he sent a six-page letter to Speaker of the House John Boehner in 2011 laying out the legal rationale. When the Supreme Court handed down its 5–4 decision in the Windsor case in 2013 that invalidated Section 3 of DOMA, marriage equality was legal in ten states. By the time of the *Obergefell* ruling exactly two years later, the number had grown to thirty-seven of the fifty states.

As these cases wended their way through the judicial system, Holder was out there as a vocal champion of LGBTQ+ rights. "And now that the Supreme Court is considering whether the Constitution guarantees marriage equality nationwide," he wrote in an op-ed for *USA Today* three months before the High Court ruled in *Obergefell*, "we have our clearest opportunity yet to mark the defining civil rights struggle of our time with triumph—a triumph of our highest ideals, our deepest values and our self-evident founding promise: that all are created equal." Those words— "the defining civil rights struggle of our time"—have extra weight coming from Holder. He is Black to his core.

With an Afro and muttonchops straight off an Afro Sheen blowout kit box, Holder and other Columbia University students staged a peaceful sit-in at a campus office to demand a meeting place for Black students. In later positions, from the bench to the helm of the Justice Department, Holder cared deeply that "liberty and justice for all" applied to "us," too. "Us," said in the way Black people say it, with a lowered voice, downturned mouth, and raised eyebrows as one of the index fingers rubs the top of the opposite hand to mean us as a people rather than a collection of intimates. So when a man with that history in Black civil rights rhetorically extended the "us" to LGBTQ+ Americans, the moral authority was clear.

The other reason I wanted Holder to officiate the wedding was I just liked him. A man who was probably that cool guy in high school everyone couldn't help liking because he exuded warmth and kindness. We have done fireside chat-style interviews in front of an audience where I pressed him on important issues, but I also found a way to get Eric to be Eric, and in the

process, I made a friend. For someone who has experienced a lot
and accomplished much, he was and remains genuinely human.

But my personal admiration for Holder was cemented
on May 30, 2013. So powerful was the moment that I raced to
Restaurant Central, a favorite dining spot and watering hole for
Justice Department employees, across Pennsylvania Avenue from
the department. There, at the long marble bar that had been my
culinary home in my early days as a New Yorker in Washington,
I wrote down what happened (and published the notes in a piece
for the paper after Holder announced his resignation in 2014).

> Holder gave me a tour of his very lived-in office. Memo-
> rabilia everywhere. Lots of pictures. One of him at Nor-
> mandy taken by his former communications director,
> Tracy Schmaler, he said, was his favorite. There is also
> a picture of himself with his favorite basketball player
> Kareem Abdul Jabbar. And there's a photo of his three
> favorite boxers, Muhammad Ali, Joe Louis and the other
> escapes me at the moment.
>
> But there was a series of four photos that caught my
> attention at his door. It was Holder interacting with a
> little boy. In one photo, Holder is seen kissing the cry-
> ing boy on the head. It was from a Drug Enforcement
> Agency memorial event in May 2009, he told me.
>
> As Holder talked about what was happening in the
> photos, his voice cracked. The family (two boys and their
> mom) was having a hard time with the loss of their father
> and her husband. The young son was too young to com-
> prehend what was going on. But, Holder said, the other

one was a little bit older and understood the gravity of losing his father.

Holder, paused several times recounting that story. Tears were visible in his eyes as we stood side by side. He was able to regain his composure. But when his press secretary Adora Jenkins asked him what he told the little boy, the halting voice and tears reappeared. He said he told the little boy that his father was a hero and that everything would eventually be okay.

On our wedding day, boutonnieres finally in place, no one seemed to know how exactly to affix them to our lapels, Nick and I and our moms descended to the lobby. We didn't circle the bend right away. The photographer gave us the cue that it was time for our moms to go to the Book Room. And then it was our turn.

The crowd of staff and onlookers in the small hallway area were a blur. I just remember smiles and applause as Nick and I made our way to our guests. Seeing them all gathered there, with broad smiles, some with hands clasped in joy, elicited from me an involuntary "Awwww!" I reached for the handkerchief in my right pocket the moment we got on the riser. I'm the crier in the family. But Holder's tears fell faster.

Coming just two weeks before Trump's inauguration, our moved-up wedding was a joyous occasion in the midst of trauma. A cathartic release after spending weeks in a state of disbelief. A mood Holder captured beautifully when he said to applause, "Nick and Jonathan, I think that that makes you official members of The Resistance. Right on!" That last exclamation punctuated by raising his left fist in the air. We weren't even halfway through our fifteen-minute ceremony when the emotion of it all hit Holder. When I heard his voice waiver, I looked over at him because I knew what was happening or about to happen.

"You want this?" I asked, offering him my blue handkerchief after having dabbed my own eyes. "I've done a lot of weddings, but this is the first time I've ever cried," Holder said as he handed it back. But more tears would follow.

My vows were really song lyrics. I took the lyrics from the first and last stanzas of the romantic song "That's All" (the Frank Sinatra version) to express my love for and hope for the future with Nick. I couldn't get through the song without crying on the treadmill or on a run. Now, standing before our friends, our moms, I couldn't get out the first few syllables without choking up.

I had longed for a day like that one. And how extraordinary it was for me to say those words to my husband in front of our mothers and in front of our friends. People who meant so much to me and to Nick, who were there when we went from "you and I" to "us." But I got there only because after years of chasing relationships and trying to wish into reality feelings that weren't there, I finally realized you can't hurry love.

CHAPTER 16

DON'T ACT LIKE YOU'VE NEVER BEEN ANYWHERE

M om was over-the-moon excited. You'd think she'd never been to the White House before. She had, a couple of times. And certainly for something more swank than this, a holiday party with the president and first lady. But this time was different.

Mom's first White House visit was back in 2000: May 22, to be exact. She came as my date to my second-ever dinner at the White House. The state dinner for South African President Thabo Mbeki hosted by President and Mrs. Clinton. The *Washington Post* story said it was "the second largest state dinner in the Clinton administration" with a receiving line that took ninety minutes to complete. More than 350 people trooped through that line to greet the Clintons and the Mbekis before exiting through the Blue Room, down the stairs of the South Portico to a waiting trolley that took them to a huge tent on the South Lawn for the seated dinner.

That we were there, part of the social mix with politicians and activists, actors and titans at the home of the president of the United States, was remarkable for both of us, but especially for Mom. Aunt Elsie once told me years later that my mother marveled to her, "Who would have thought a girl from Severn would have dinner at the White House?" And I could sense her building excitement, which was why, as we put the finishing touches on our respective black-tie attire, I explained the import of the evening. I reminded my mother that we weren't going to Disney World so she shouldn't expect me to be taking pictures all over the place. Next, I impressed upon her that because I was a journalist who was just beginning to do television, this was work. More importantly, though, it was imperative that we act like we belong there, unfazed by the people and the history that would surround us.

Mom told me she got it. "We can't act like we've never been anywhere," she said, employing a bit of down-home Black wisdom. Because folks who've "never been anywhere" don't know how to act. They usually end up embarrassing themselves when thrust into a situation with "proper comp'ny." And you can't get more proper than the "comp'ny" at a White House state dinner. I was relieved to hear her say those words. Words that were promptly forgotten the moment she entered the East Wing.

We alighted from our town car and walked in behind Sandy Thurman, Clinton's AIDS Czar, who exited her town car like Cinderella arriving at the ball, a cloud of a white gown trailing her forward motion onto the sidewalk of East Executive Avenue and up the steps to the East Portico. Mom's resolve to "act right" dissolved upon seeing the collection of famous guests with whom she was rubbing elbows. The exclamations came in rapid succession. "There's Harry Belafonte!" "There's Stevie Wonder!" "There's John Lewis!" Every so often, she would throw in, "This is Black history! Black history!"

Then there was the constant "take my picture" that I intermittently refused with an increasing irritation, which bubbled over after I escorted her to her table under the tent. "Take all the pictures you want," I said, thrusting her camera back into her hands before heading to my table.

Georgia Representative John Lewis, the civil rights icon whose courage and leadership helped make it possible for the two of us to share such a special evening in such an august place, was a few seats to my right. The wife of Republican Senator Orrin Hatch of Utah was there. So, too, was Capricia Penavic Marshall, the same White House social secretary who stunned me eight months earlier on the receiving line at the dinner for the recipients of the National Medal of the Arts and the National Humanities Medal by saying, "You know you're sitting at the president's table?" A gorgeous and gracious wisp of a woman who looked every bit the part she played. So gracious that when I returned from checking on my mom at her table, Capricia insisted that they swap seats during dessert. My anger gone, I told Mom to look at who was sitting at the table directly behind her.

Vice President Al Gore was infinitely more engaging, approachable, and human in person than he presented on television. I learned this over a few encounters with him in the months leading up to the state dinner. The first time being at his daughter Karenna's Manhattan apartment the previous year. This explains why I felt comfortable saying to Mom, "Come with me." Tapping him on the shoulder, I said hello to the vice president and then with all the faux exasperation I could muster, I asked, "Would you MIND taking a picture with my mother?" Gore popped up from his seat without hesitation, greeted my mother, and locked on to her for the photo. "He put his arm around me tight," she squealed the next morning as we recounted our favorite moments of the memorable evening. She thrilled at President Clinton saying to her after being introduced, "Your son likes to come here from time to time." And she gushed and giggled about First Lady Hillary Clinton swooning to Mrs. Mbeki about how young Mom looked. She couldn't possibly be my mother, they said.

The White House holiday party on December 9, 2011, was altogether different. A different kind of Black history.

President and Mrs. Obama were hosting the print press that night, and Mom was my date. America's first Black president had been in office for nearly three years. By then, I'd met Obama a few times. Heard him speak at length about you name the policy. Been awed and proud that someone who looked like me, an exemplar of the character I hoped to exhibit, was the leader of the free world. Mom had only seen and heard him on television. And now she was about to meet him. Shake his hand. Talk to him. Take a photo with him—and Mrs. Obama.

Jeremy Bernard found us somewhere on the State Floor of the White House and brought us down to the ground floor, where we would get our announcement card and wait in line. Jeremy was the White House social secretary. A dear friend who I'd met through Broadway and movie producer Scott Sanders, another friend who lived in New York. Jeremy and his then-partner, Rufus Gifford, were among the first to help Obama in his presidential quest in California. Jeremy's reward was a series of presidential appointments, including chief of staff to the American ambassador to France. We were having brunch at one of our favorite meeting spots in Washington, Hank's Oyster Bar, during a leave from Paris when he said, "I have a meeting with the first lady." I shrieked, "Get out!" because I knew what it meant. The job of social secretary was open with the departure of Julianna Smoot, and Mrs. Obama was looking for her replacement. From the moment he said it, I knew the job was his. He was perfect for it, bringing a keen political sense to a job that tapped his creativity. And now Jeremy was leading us to the Map Room to queue up in the photo line.

The military social aide requested our announcement card and double-checked the pronunciation of our names. "Margaret Kindred Capehart," he said, asking if she wanted all three names said. Mom said, "Just Margaret Capehart." I stopped the Marine and said, "Please say all three names." Mom looked at me with familiar irritation. "I don't want all three names said," she said sternly. I repeated my request to the Marine and thanked him. As he walked away, Mom, sparkling in the dress I bought her for her seventieth birthday dinner at the Four Seasons restaurant in New York a few weeks earlier, turned to me. She wanted to know why I was so insistent on having her maiden name said. "Because I want the Kindred name said in the White House," I told her. "I want the president of the United States to hear the family name."

After one more check by social staff and handing over her purse so her hands were free for the photo, Mom and I made our way into the Diplomatic Reception Room, where the president and first lady took photos with one couple after another at a clip of about twenty seconds each. We were two couples away from our turn with the Obamas, now standing single file in the order we would be announced when I looked back, and I'll never forget what I saw.

The girl from Severn who was raised during the racial segregation of Jim Crow, the proud Black mother who had raised her son to do well and prayed that he would, the proud African American woman who, like generations before her, hoped that one day her nation would elect a Black president who symbolized the best of her people, but believed in her bones that her country would do no such thing, was mere steps away from a dream come true.

Mom didn't seem to notice I was looking at her. Her gaze was set on the Obamas as if her eyes had locked on to a pair of unicorns, a pair of fantastic beings she'd thought she'd never see in her lifetime. And yet there they were, standing under a portrait of George Washington in front of a fireplace decked out with a garland made of magnolia leaves and ornaments. David Wildman, hired by Jeremy to design the White House just so, told me his team "tried to pick up the colors that would work with and highlight the wallpaper Jackie Kennedy put in the Diplomatic Room." The deep blues and highlights of purple and white reflected a desire, he said, to not "go too overboard as we wanted to make sure whatever FLOTUS wore, it would look nice against the color palette." The first lady was stunning in a chic spaghetti-strapped ivory-colored dress, which blended in nicely with the surrounding ornaments. Her long, dangling earrings echoed those on the Christmas trees on either side of her and the president, who looked handsome in his navy blue suit and blue tie.

"Jonathan Capehart and Margaret Kindred Capehart," came the announcement.

I greeted the president and then made my way to the first lady. As Mom approached them close behind me, her foot caught on the carpet and she nearly fell. But the President swooped in, saving her from going down. "I got you," he reassured her. I don't remember what else was said. Usually, no one ever does. The encounter is too fast, the company too intimidating, to remember anything other than walking into and out of the room. But our fleeting moment was captured by the White House photographer, and you can see the power of it on Mom's face. Her eyes sparkle. Her smile broad and bright. She is among the unicorns and she is in awe.

—————

That was in 2011, and it would not be her last time at the White House queuing up to take a photo with the Obamas. My plus-one to the White House holiday party for the press alternated between my mother and Nick so she came with me again in 2013 and 2015. For her, each time was as exciting as the first. Mom loved everything about the Obamas during their White House years. She loved what they represented. She loved how they represented "us." And because of that, the Obamas, as a couple and individually, had an enormous impact on how she saw herself and issues. I often quipped that if President Obama supported it and Mrs. Obama wore it, my mother was all for it. But it was true.

Vice President Biden was the one who went on *Meet the Press* on May 6, 2012, and declared, "I am absolutely comfortable with the fact that men marrying men, women marrying women, and heterosexual men and women marrying are entitled to the same exact rights, all the civil rights, all the civil liberties." His comments set off a firestorm because he got ahead of President Obama, who then sat with ABC News's Robin Roberts three days later to announce, "It is important for me to go ahead and affirm that—I think same-sex couples should be able to get married."

The true power of a president, the ability to change minds and hearts simply by expressing support for an issue, was brought home to me over Mother's Day brunch later that week. Under an umbrella on the terrace at Blue Duck Tavern, I asked my born-again Christian mom, whose evolution on gay issues, especially same-sex marriage, seemed grudgingly slow, what she thought about what Obama said about gay marriage. She said she agreed with him and then said it was "cruel" to deny same-sex couples the rights and responsibilities that accrue to marriage. She kept coming back to the possibility of an estranged family swooping in to take the home away from a surviving spouse simply because the state would not allow the couple to marry and cloak them in the legal protections that come with it. I sat in stunned amazement, recognizing that Obama's public change of position gave Mom permission to do the same.

As for Mrs. Obama, over the years, Mom would tell me about the things she saw the first lady wear, commenting on how beautiful she looked. And that's no lie. Mrs. Obama makes even the simplest, financially accessible garment look chic, magical. No wonder whatever she wore sold out. Folks wanted some of her magic for themselves. More than once, a meet-up with Mom led to her pointing out with a smile which part of her outfit was inspired by "Michelle." She'd say it with such pride.

Mom always likes to look good when stepping out in public, but she took extra care when she knew she was going to the White House to see the Obamas. She had to look better than good for them. Everything had to be perfect. And Mom looked perfect when we arrived for the 2015 holiday press party. Beautiful in her Eliza J dress made of black lace with off-white underlay. In her black kitten heels, Mom looked very chic.

Mom knew the drill as we made our way once again to the Diplomatic Reception Room for the prized photo with the First Couple. She handed over her black clutch for retrieval after the meet-and-greet and then stood behind me as my name would be called first on the receiving line. When President Obama and Mrs. Obama came into view, Mom said excitedly, "I'm wearing the same dress as Michelle! I'm wearing the same dress as Michelle!" Sure enough, I turned around to see the first lady standing regally in a very similar dress, black lace with an underlay in black and gold. The two of them thrilled at being fashion twins. "I was dressed like Michelle Obama!" Mom said repeatedly as we made our way home.

The last Obama White House function I attended with my mother was epic. The kind of epic that they take your cell phones upon arrival in the East Wing lobby. So epic that an administration official told me that a friend of hers also in attendance called his grandmother on his predawn drive back home. When she asked for details, he said, "Gather the children!"

It started as a relatively simple affair. The taping of *Love and Happiness: An Obama Celebration* for BET was held on the South Lawn under a tent that had been erected for the October 18, 2016, state dinner for Italian Prime Minister Matteo Renzi, where I had been television host Tamron Hall's plus-one three nights earlier. After performances by Jill Scott, Common, Janelle Monáe, Leslie Odom Jr., The Roots, De La Soul, Bell Biv Devoe, Usher, and a gospel number from Yolanda Adams, Michelle Williams, and Kierra Sheard that had us singing along and on our feet most of the time, the president jokingly thanked BET "for agreeing to film Barack Obama's Block Party." We all laughed, but that's exactly what erupted back in the East Room.

The star-studded guests had the run of the place after the concert. Eating, drinking, and having a good ol' time throughout the State Floor of the White House. Mom and I made our way to the East Room after getting a bite to eat. DJ D-Nice was spinning tunes near the southern wall. Mom and I joined others in dancing, but she was having such a good time that I ended up standing by a wall holding her purse.

Mom gets this look on her face when she's ready to leave. I could see it and suggested we go. We'd had a good time. But as we were starting to make our way out, a song came on that took Mom way back. I'm almost certain it was Stevie Wonder's "Do I Do." A quintessential barbecue song guaranteed to pull even the most dog-tired out to the dance floor. And there my mother went and stayed for more than an hour. Dancing like she did when she was younger. This time I'm holding her purse and her shoes.

With supermodel Naomi Campbell swaying her hips and hair next to him, D-Nice kept the pace moving, and next thing I know, I'm watching Mom and a couple hundred other people bopping in unison to DMX's "Party Up (Up in Here)"and "Swag Surfin'" by Fast Life Yungstaz as George and Martha Washington stoically watched from their portraits on the east wall.

Then, when President Obama came into the center of the room with Janelle Monáe and others, my seventy-five-year-old mother moved with the swiftness of Florence Griffith Joyner in the 100-meter. Mom put her hands on the man standing between her and the action unfolding just beyond her reach. She tried moving him to her right, then to her left. She only let go after I told her rather urgently that the man the size of a Sub-Zero and just as immovable was a Secret Service agent.

We didn't leave until after 1:00 a.m.

In those moments, I'm not just taking in the immediate action unfolding before my eyes. I'm overlaying all the history that propelled us to that moment. I can't help thinking that we are a long way from 175 North First Street in Newark or the painful stepfather years. And I can't help thinking about the girl from Severn, North Carolina. Like so many Black women past, present, and future, my mother made a way out of no way. She struggled and sacrificed to lodge me on the path that led to grand nights like those. Nights where acting like you've never been anywhere is actually one of the purest expressions of joy there is.

CHAPTER 17

"WHAT TIMES WE'RE GOING TO HAVE"

One of my favorite movies is *Auntie Mame*, the 1958 film in which Rosalind Russell plays Mame Dennis. The movie begins with the avant-garde heiress throwing one of her extravagant parties in 1920s New York City when, after the sudden death of her brother, her nephew Patrick Dennis arrives in the middle of the affair.

Mame is thrilled to see her nephew but is appalled by his limited vocabulary and what that reveals about the limitations of his understanding of the world. Then she utters the line that never fails to make me tear up: "Your Auntie Mame's going to open doors for you, Patrick. Doors you never even dreamed existed. Oh, what times we're going to have." I get emotional because I know what's coming. At the end of the movie, Mame convinces Patrick to allow his grade school son Michael to travel with her to India. While leading him up her grand Beekman Place staircase, Mame repeats the same lines she once said to his father. Generation upon generation, discovering the world anew.

That discovery can only happen if you "live!" Another one of Mame's mantras. But it has an important addition: "Life is a banquet and most poor suckers are starving to death!" That mantra has nothing to do with wealth. Having the wherewithal to not have to care about your bank balance is literally a luxury most everyone doesn't have. Availing yourself of life's banquet requires gumption. The greatest lives are those centered around the people we consider family, the places where we are our truest selves, or the things that evoke the most cherished memories.

I have years of music playlists whose songs can take me back to a specific place, a specific time, a specific mood or emotion. My Rome 2019 playlist is music I heard while listening to Brian Delp on jazz station WBGO during my early morning, pre-heatwave walks in the Eternal City during a month-long stay writing another version of this book. My Rome 2024 playlist has songs I heard around me while spending a few days in Rome writing this version of the book. The original playlist that has been a soundtrack of my life is one created by Ron Norsworthy for Ada Tola's thirtieth birthday entitled "LaGlarmorada," a compilation of moody music that takes me back to the late 1990s, early 2000s. The days of pork chops and martinis at Restaurant Florent, roof parties on Little West 12th Street, and reading the Sunday papers on the beach.

If you're lucky, you are living your best life with the people in the places and alongside the things that bring you the greatest joy.

Unfortunately, far too many people struggle with achieving just one of the three. And the older I get, the more I see how people are depleted of the gumption to "live!" The seemingly innocuous comments that sow seeds of doubt. The people who put a ceiling on others' dreams by telling them they can't do something and, when they defy the odds and do it, then tell them not to get too big for their britches. And then there's self-sabotage, the surest sign that we are the ones standing in the way of what we want, what would let us "live!"

This doesn't mean you won't hit obstacles, fail, or be disappointed. As someone who has hit all three, I can tell you that's what life's banquet is all about. Triumphing over them is what makes whatever success you achieve, however you define it, that much sweeter.

My life is filled with people who are more than friends. They are family. Darren Walker. Joe Versace. Valerie Jarrett. Karen Finney. People who give me that intangible feeling of home and the safety and accountability that come with it. Thanks to Giuseppe, I found home in Italy, a nation whose entire way of being could be boiled down to "live!" And it is one of two places where I feel most myself, where my shoulders rest. The other is Martha's Vineyard, that magical island off Cape Cod that has a strong indigenous and African American history.

When Nick and I went to the Vineyard for the first time together, I observed something that was at once marvelous and sad. I thrilled at seeing so many Black people and Black families on vacation. Riding bikes. Going to the beach. Dining out. Black children being children, carefree. Sad, because even making those observations demonstrates how rare it is to see "Us" at peace.

Valerie Jarrett and her cousin Ann Walker Marchant, who threw a welcome to Washington party when I first moved to town, told me several times over the years, "You should come to the Vineyard." They and their extended family have been going for generations. Having spent several summers there, I now understand that to be told to come to the Vineyard is to be told to come home.

That word: home. I discovered how important it is to me while writing this book. I come back to it again and again in these pages. I have found it in people and places and things. When "home" is present, the possibilities are limitless. And nothing represents limitless possibilities like the promise of America. It is what has made the United States a beacon of hope and opportunity for people around the world.

In October 2018, the middle of the Trump presidency, I was in Amsterdam for a speech. I happened to notice the lock-screen photo of one of my hosts. It was of the Statue of Liberty. At that moment, a chill went through me, for it was a glorious reminder that the Lady in the Harbor, that symbol of freedom and America, still meant something to people around the world.

———————

As ever, the American people are on a forward march. It's incremental and painfully slow. But the destination is a glorious one: a more perfect union. This is what undergirds my enduring faith in this nation even when this nation puts that faith to the test on a daily basis.

That was especially so during the Trump years, when everything turned upside down. When Republicans junked decades of norms and long-held beliefs to fall in line with the authoritarianism and white nationalism of a wealthy Queens-born builder masquerading as an of-the-people populist. Like many Americans, I was in despair over what was happening to my country, what continues to happen.

But in his epic Pulitzer Prize–winning biography of Frederick Douglass, Yale history professor David Blight wrote a passage that was simple in its execution but sweeping in its scope and gave me the perspective I needed and still rely on to give me the hope that we will get through this.

> The orator and writer lived to see and interpret black emancipation, to work actively for women's rights long before they were achieved, to realize the civil rights triumphs and tragedies of Reconstruction, and to witness and contribute to America's economic and international expansion in the Gilded Age. He lived to the age of lynching and Jim Crow laws, when America collapsed into retreat from the very victories and revolutions in race relations he had helped to win.

What gave me hope in Blight's words was the sweep of Douglass's life. A man who was born a slave and escaped, who was a celebrated orator against the sin of slavery and saw the end of that evil institution. Douglass played a part in the nation reaching toward its founding ideals during Reconstruction. And then the great man lived long enough to see all the gains he fought for be reversed by Congress, the courts, and the president during the terror of the Jim Crow era. My story is proof that Douglass's fight was not lost. That as bad as things are, they won't stay that way.

I am a descendant of slaves, whose parents were born and raised in the segregated Jim Crow South. My cousins and I are the first generation in our family who didn't have to pick cotton. My story is the story of an only child mama's boy who had dreams of being a journalist and no road map for how to achieve them. I'm a Black man who writes for the *Washington Post*, anchors a show on MSNBC, and serves as a political analyst on *PBS NewsHour*. And I am an out gay man who was able to marry the man I love and have the ceremony officiated by the attorney general of the United States who made a key determination that made it possible.

"A more perfect Union" we do not yet have. But notice how the framers crafted that phrase in the Preamble of the Constitution. "A more perfect Union" in and of itself is an aspiration. A destination that is never quite reached. For a perfect Union can never be achieved as long as people are left out, are not allowed to fully participate. Through our individual acts and collective action, we the people make this a more perfect union.

I firmly believe this because my story is a testament to it. Hard work and the gumption to push through doors I never dreamed existed put me on a path to meet people I never should have met in a life that I never should have been able to live. Statistics and popular myth say Black boys like me don't reach these heights. And yet here I am.

ACKNOWLEDGMENTS

Everything we do in life is an audition for something else.

My work as an editorial writer in New York resulted in my meeting with Fred Hiatt at the *Washington Post*. To prepare, I read Katharine Graham's autobiography, *Personal History*, which won the Pulitzer Prize for Biography in 1998.

What impressed me more than her story was how Mrs. Graham told it. She was honest and transparent in ways I never thought possible for someone of her stature. Fast-forward to 2014 and the publication of Charles Blow's memoir, *Shut Up in My Bones*. I read that too and was struck by Charles's raw and honest recounting of his life. It put into perspective the passion that fueled every one of his columns for the *New York Times*.

Mrs. Graham and Charles couldn't be more different. But in their respective memoirs, they were willing to be introspective and vulnerable on the page. I knew that if I were ever to write a book, their example would be my guide. I'd turn the lens of introspection on myself and be honest about what I learned. I'd share my triumphs and my failures. I'd share my story hoping that someone would see some part of themselves or their experience in it.

In 2023, the publisher of Twelve Books, Sean Desmond, sent me an email asking if I'd ever thought about writing a book. Thanks to Katharine Graham and Charles Blow, not only had I thought about writing a book, I had already started working on one.

I first put pen to paper in the early months of the first Trump administration, when I needed an escape. I took Nick's advice and began recounting all the stories from my youth, teen years, and later life—the good, bad, and ugly. And then I asked Tamron Hall, April Ryan, and Joy Reid to read what I'd written. So it was their initial encouragement, too, that got me started and kept me going.

Sean's departure to another publishing house placed me in the kind and careful hands of Colin Dickerman at Grand Central Publishing. I cannot thank Colin and the Grand Central team enough for all they did to turn this dream into reality. I also owe a thousand thanks to my literary agent, Gail Ross, and my television agent, Olivia Metzger, who insisted I talk to Gail before doing anything. And a special thank-you to Paul Bogaards for his incredible guidance in maximizing my storytelling and the reach of this book, and to Beowulf Sheehan for his cover portrait and, more important, for suggesting "Yet Here I Am" as a title.

In some ways, this book is one long acknowledgment—its more than 250 pages are filled with gratitude for the many who've helped me along the way. But there were others whose friendship, love, and kindness I could always count on. They include Samantha Tubman and Joe Paulsen, Jeffrey Martin, Kirk and Crystal Wagar, Christine Taylor, Holly Peterson, Carol Wu, Nana Efua Smith, Tamron Hall and Steven Greener, Greg Kordick, Dan Bauman, Kamala Harris and Doug Emhoff, Michael Shea and Ed McClellan, Lawrence O'Donnell, Juliet Johnson, Kevin Baron and Sharon Stirling, David Sokol, Laura Jarrett, Robert

Raben, Jordan Roth and Richie Jackson, Serena Torrey Roosevelt, Mariapaola and Giancarlo Scognamiglio, Mario and Tina Lignano, Chris Jansing, Rick Angellar, Vickee Jordan Adams, Cidney White, Bob Barnett, Aaron Polkey and Jason Coleman, Steve Aiello, Sandra Stevenson, Alexandra Stanton and Sam Natapoff, David Meadvin, Lynn Forester de Rothschild, Brian Ellner, Mark Walsh and Brian Rafanelli, James Holm, Fred Hochberg and Tom Healy, Katherine O'Hearn, Hilary Rosen, Jesse Rodriguez, Ali Velshi, my show teams at MSNBC and Post Live, and the great team at *PBS NewsHour*.

I owe a special thanks to the people and places that gave me sanctuaries in which to write and reflect. The Hamilton Box at the lounge of Blue Duck Tavern (Alyssa, Donte, Michael, and Luis); the J.K. Place Roma; Borgo Finocchieto; Mario Maffezzoni's wonderful apartment and rooftop terrace in Trastevere, Rome; Chris Jansing's stunning patio in Tuscany; the Salamander Middleburg in Virginia, the Ivy Hotel Baltimore, and Holly Peterson's red dining room on Park Avenue.

I also want to give a special thank-you to some online admirers who have been cheering me on—and in many instances, defending me—since the dawn of social media: Nancy Lee Krieger, Kim Giordano, Steve Beste, Robert Hill, Renee Rouse-Rousseau, @mwj1231, @nicaforpeace, @dovescorner, @bzthomasb, and Jill E. Bond. I am honored by their faith in me.

Finally, I want to thank YOU, dear reader. This book is everything to me. I hope you liked it and have gotten to know me a little better by having read it.

ABOUT THE AUTHOR

Jonathan Capehart is a Pulitzer Prize–winning journalist and associate editor at the *Washington Post*, where he is also an opinion writer and anchor for *Washington Post Live*. He is also anchor of *The Saturday Show* and *The Sunday Show* on MSNBC. His MSNBC special *A Promised Land: A Conversation with Barack Obama* was nominated in 2021 for an Emmy for Outstanding News Discussion & Analysis. He is also an analyst on *The PBS NewsHour*.